MAKE WORK OPTIONAL

MAKE WORK OPTIONAL
Life Lessons for Today's Investor

JONATHON C. LEISE

BALBOA
PRESS
A DIVISION OF HAY HOUSE

Copyright © 2015 Jonathon C. Leise.

All rights reserved. No part of this book may be used or reproduced by any means, graphic, electronic, or mechanical, including photocopying, recording, taping or by any information storage retrieval system without the written permission of the publisher except in the case of brief quotations embodied in critical articles and reviews.

Balboa Press books may be ordered through booksellers or by contacting:

Balboa Press
A Division of Hay House
1663 Liberty Drive
Bloomington, IN 47403
www.balboapress.com
1 (877) 407-4847

Because of the dynamic nature of the Internet, any web addresses or links contained in this book may have changed since publication and may no longer be valid. The views expressed in this work are solely those of the author and do not necessarily reflect the views of the publisher, and the publisher hereby disclaims any responsibility for them.

The author of this book does not dispense medical advice or prescribe the use of any technique as a form of treatment for physical, emotional, or medical problems without the advice of a physician, either directly or indirectly. The intent of the author is only to offer information of a general nature to help you in your quest for emotional and spiritual well-being. In the event you use any of the information in this book for yourself, which is your constitutional right, the author and the publisher assume no responsibility for your actions.

Any people depicted in stock imagery provided by Thinkstock are models, and such images are being used for illustrative purposes only.
Certain stock imagery © Thinkstock.

Printed in the United States of America.

ISBN: 978-1-5043-2650-6 (sc)
ISBN: 978-1-5043-2652-0 (hc)
ISBN: 978-1-5043-2651-3 (e)

Library of Congress Control Number: 2015900625

Balboa Press rev. date: 01/26/2015

CONTENTS

Introduction ix

Chapter 1 Lessons Learned 1
    My Passion 1
    In the Beginning 2

Chapter 2 Investor No-No's 23
    No Plan 25
    No Process 27
    No Idea 31
    No Purpose 33

Chapter 3 Mistakes to Avoid at All Costs 37
    Mistake #1: Great Expectations 37
    Mistake #2: Fighting the Last War 46
    Mistake # 3: Believing the Current Hype ... 61
    Mistake #4: Not Paying for Protection 72
    I Have Your Back—Always 77
    Other Mistakes to Avoid 84

Chapter 4   Making Work Optional 87
   Special Risks Around Retirement. 87
   The Riskiest Day of Your Life. 87
   Sometimes There Is No Tomorrow 90
   Serious Mistakes 97
   Retirement Risk #1: Longevity 99
   Retirement Risk #2: Sequence of Returns. 102
   Retirement Risk #3: Reverse Dollar-Cost Averaging. 106
   Retirement Risk # 4: Complacency 109
   Retirement Risk #5: The Black Swan Event 113
   Retirement Risk #6: Not Paying for Protection—Again . . .116
   In Summary 124

Chapter 5   The Best Investment 125

INTRODUCTION

If you are a man, woman, or couple trying to raise a family, pay your bills, and accumulate enough financial assets to eventually make work optional, read this book. If you are beginning to save or have just inherited a financial windfall, this book is for you. If you are an employee or union member accumulating money in your annuity, 401(k), 403(b), or pension, pay attention to the principles discussed. If you are a business owner or executive with a busy schedule trying to do the right thing for your employees and build significant net worth for yourself, you will benefit from this book. If you have found yourself facing a financial windfall, such as:

- Retirement plan rollover,
- Sale of a business,
- Inheritance or large gift,
- Lottery win,
- Professional sports contract,
- Major career advancement, or
- Divorce settlement,

then this book is for you.

This book is meant to be both an inspiration and a road map to live a successful, rewarding life and to reach your potential spiritually, psychologically, and financially. As the motivational speakers and preachers I have listened to and gained inspiration from like to say, "This book will change your life!" In fact, if you learn enough to avoid some of the serious mistakes many people make and get on the road to financial freedom, it may change your life—maybe not dramatically at first, but significantly over time.

You can either learn from your own mistakes or you can save yourself the aggravation and learn from the mistakes of others. Over the last thirty-plus years in the financial services business, I have seen some of the most devastating mistakes made over and over and wish to save you the aggravation. Financial lessons we learn the hard way are costly—and not just in dollars and cents. I mean "costly" in the sense that financial lessons learned the hard way often rob us of years, even decades, of our precious time. They set us back, hold us back, and prevent us from reaching our full potential and living life to the fullest. Most costly of all, financial lessons and mistakes will rob millions of Americans of the opportunity to retire and live comfortably through their golden years.

If you were driving along the road and someone came running from up ahead, all bloody and scratched, and stopped to tell you the bridge was out, what would you do? If you would tell him to mind his own business and get out of your way, you can skip this book. But if you would be willing to learn from the mistakes of others and find another way to get where you were going, then read on!

Who am I, and why should you listen to me? I am a person with a passion for my craft and a commitment to excellence in my chosen field. I entered the financial services industry in 1980, and since that time I have been a "student of the game," reading and studying the habits of successful people—and watching and taking note of the mistakes made by not-so-successful people. I want you to be successful, so I illustrate some of the most common and costly mistakes and explain the most important risks to a successful retirement. I do this with stories and anecdotes taken from the quarterly newsletters I have been writing for my clients, beginning in 1994. I hope you enjoy what I have written from the heart.

CHAPTER ONE

Lessons Learned

MY PASSION

I love what I do for a living. I get to help investors accumulate wealth, protect that wealth, and distribute that wealth. I have the privilege of helping them provide for their families, save for retirement, and generate income to pay their bills in their later years. In order to earn that privilege, I endured decades of hard work to build my business and establish trust, while raising a family of my own. It was hard work—and still is.

I began to write and issue a quarterly client newsletter in 1994, six years before the "lost decade" began, and fourteen years before the financial crisis and great recession of 2008. I have looked back on those newsletters, and I believe that the investment and life principles discussed were sound then and remain sound now. I tried to keep my clients up-to-date on what was happening with my family, teach them investment principles, calm them during difficult times, and inspire them in general.

This book includes anecdotes from those newsletters, with color commentary to fill the gaps. It is meant to entertain you with stories about my family, my experiences, and current events; teach investment principles; and inspire people to live better lives. Newsletter excerpts have remained pretty much intact to illustrate the points I try to make. I hope you benefit as much as I have enjoyed sharing.

IN THE BEGINNING ...

I grew up in a small town and went to the same high school as my parents, who were a baker and a housewife. I had no idea that we were not rich. My father worked at night and coached Little League and attended all of my baseball and football games. My mother was a stay-at-home mom who did not drive. They loved each other, and I felt loved and supported by them. My father taught me to work as hard as I could and to always do my best because you never know who might be watching. My mother taught me to always do the right thing ... because you never know who might be watching! As detailed in my newsletter from the spring of 2014:

> ### American Hustle
>
> In the Academy Award-nominated movie American Hustle, a highly fictionalized telling of the bizarre Abscam FBI corruption sting of the 1970s, the public official on the take is the most selfless character. In the film, Mayor Carmine Polito turns down, and then accepts, a briefcase full of money he is offered as a bribe. The character, based on real-life Camden, New Jersey, Mayor Angelo Errichetti, believes doing so would lead to job production and help residents.
>
> Before he was mayor of Camden, Errichetti was a talented running back for Camden High School, winning the

Brooks-Irvine Memorial Football Club's South Jersey Back of the Year. The following year, that award went to Vineland's Eugene Caterina. Vineland played at Collingswood that year, and near the end of the game Eugene broke free down the sideline for what appeared to be the winning touchdown. As he approached the end zone, out of nowhere, from the other side of the field came a hustling #7 for Collingswood, Conrad Leise, who caught him at the three-yard line and hit him with such force he almost landed in the stadium seats! Collingswood went on to win the game; Conrad was named the Brooks-Irvine Club's Lineman of the Year and later was included on the All-Time All-South Jersey football team. And, as everyone in the family knows, the grass is always green on the three-yard line at Collingswood High School.

Later that year, Diane Carson, a cheerleader, asked Conrad Leise to the Sadie Hawkins Dance at Collingswood. Seven years later, on Valentine's Day, they were married in Collingswood. Two years later, they welcomed Jonathon Carson Leise to the world and later had two more children, Cindy and Mark.

Playing on the same field as my father, I did not achieve my goal of winning the Brooks-Irvine Club Player of the Year. I did, however, avenge his only loss by beating Haddonfield in every football game I played against them and, like him, was inducted into the Collingswood High School Athletic Hall of Fame. This past Valentine's weekend my daughter, Jael, was married in Collingswood to complete the circle. My sister, Cindy, was the wedding planner. My brother and fellow hall of famer, Mark, did the reading. My good friend Pastor Rick, also a member of the Collingswood Athletic

Hall of Fame, performed the ceremony. The date, location, and participants made it special for me, but the best part is that my baby girl found the right man and is happy.

Upon graduation from high school, I went to college, intent on becoming a lawyer. I worked several jobs to pay my way through. Whenever I was home, I worked on the back of a trash truck, or on the "prestigious" tree crew. In the summers I also painted houses and cut lawns after the trash was picked up. At school, I gave campus tours and did odd jobs, from pulling weeds to tending bar. I also sold my plasma at a local blood bank for $16 a week. I played football and baseball and joined a fraternity. When I found out that room and board was free for the treasurer of the fraternity, I ran and was elected to the position. I lived in the frat house during my junior and senior years. I finished college with a degree in accounting and no job.

When I graduated from college—the first of my generation in my family to do so—I was too broke to pay for the application fees for law school. So I spent several days going into every office building in the Philadelphia/South Jersey area seeking a job. I then began working as a dishwasher at a local restaurant. After two weeks, I received a job offer from one of the companies I had visited, and I accepted while standing in the kitchen of the restaurant. I became a financial analyst for RCA Service Company, pricing government contracts. While I was there, I got involved in an investment club with a group of coworkers and began to develop an interest in stocks.

I got friendly with the broker who serviced our account and thought it might be a good career. Since the company provided tuition reimbursement, I also started going to school at night to get an MBA. One of the courses I took was on investments, taught by the director of research for a local stock brokerage firm. He was a great guy and we hit it off, and I once again thought I might want to get into the brokerage business. Looking back, meeting this gentleman changed my life then and produced profound changes later. This turned out to be one of many examples of God looking out for me and my family.

From the Fall 2005 newsletter:

My Hero

After earning a degree in accounting from Franklin & Marshall College in 1977, the next logical step for me was to take advantage of my employer's offer to pay for me to get my MBA. So I began going to Drexel University at night. Since a few of my coworkers and I had begun an investment club, I took a course in investments. I found the subject actually to be interesting, and the professor was a real broker. He was funny, interesting, and knowledgeable. In addition, he was opinionated, and his opinions seemed to match mine. He seemed like a genuinely good man whom I would like to be like when I "grew up." His name was Paul Hagerty.

My brief association with Mr. Hagerty led me to pursue a career in investments. I called on him to help me get in the door, which he graciously did. I made the right career choice and have now been at it for twenty-five years. In 1992, I joined Janney Montgomery Scott (also a good choice) and could not believe that in the office next to mine was none other than Paul Hagerty. We have become friends; I admire him and even consider him my hero, a man of integrity and character. Now I am proud to be his partner. We will be working together as a team to provide customized solutions to your individual needs and objectives. (Paul has since retired, and I continue to serve his former clients.)

I was introduced to a single mother by a coworker and soon fell in love with both her and her daughter. On our first date we talked about end-times prophecy, and she was fascinated. Before we went into the restaurant, I asked her to kiss me to get it out of the way and to avoid any awkwardness later. She luckily complied, and our romance was under way.

Following our second date, when I asked to see her again, she balked and indicated that she wanted to take things slowly. I sat her down and informed her that she and I were going to get married and she might as well get used to the idea. She cried and sort of agreed that it might happen and agreed to go out with me again. We were married six months later and shortly thereafter had a second daughter. Debby left her job to raise the kids, and we struggled financially. We then made two very important decisions. First, we felt that it was important to tithe 10 percent of our income to the local church. We believed that this act of obedience would invite financial blessing. (We continue to tithe to this day and firmly believe it is the most important contributor to my financial success.) I also decided to take the leap into the 100 percent commission world of stock brokerage. It was a chance to make considerably more money (eventually!) while getting into a field that I found interesting, and helping people while I was at it. But first I had to make less money while I was building a clientele.

It was a big risk, the first of many I would take, but my wife supported me, and I was not afraid to put in the work necessary to succeed. I borrowed some money to pay a consultant to teach me how to interview and landed a position with Dean Witter. It was harder than it looked—it still is—but slowly people began to give me a chance and a book of business began to evolve.

From the Summer 2006 newsletter:

ONE QUARTER CENTURY AGO

Twenty-five years ago, in 1981, John Smith—who is now in the mutual fund business—sank a layup with only seconds remaining to vault St. Joseph's University to a 49–48 victory over number-one ranked DePaul University and into the Sweet Sixteen of the NCAA men's basketball tournament. Footage of the celebration following the game shows head coach Jim Lynam being hugged by his young daughter, Dei, who can be seen these days on Comcast SportsNet. The Hawks went on to the Elite Eight, where they were defeated by the eventual NCAA champion Indiana Hoosiers. Indiana was coached by Bob Knight and led by sophomore point guard Isiah Thomas, the current New York Knicks coach.

The final game between Indiana and North Carolina was played at the Spectrum in Philadelphia. Earlier that day, President Ronald Reagan was shot and, as he was being wheeled into surgery, told his wife Nancy, "I forgot to duck!" No one knew how serious his condition was until after he was out of surgery and out of danger. The Academy Awards ceremony was postponed a day, but the basketball game went on. After the game, reporting from Washington for NBC News, John Palmer quoted a message the President had scribbled in his hospital room shortly after surgery. "All in all," Reagan had written, borrowing W. C. Fields' line, "I'd rather be in Philadelphia."

That same year, former Philadelphia Eagles head coach Joe Kuharich passed away while future head coach Andy Reid married his wife, Tammy. Herman Munster (Fred Gwynne) also got married that year to his second wife, Deb. In an apparent mismatch, heavy metal rocker Eddie Van Halen married *One Day at a Time* cutie Valerie Bertinelli. That marriage lasted longer than most predicted. Working Girl Melanie Griffith took a break between her two marriages to *Miami Vice*'s Don Johnson, to marry Steve Bauer (Al Pacino's sidekick in *Scarface*). She is now married to Zorro (Antonio Banderas). The most watched wedding that year, or any year, was that of H.R.H. Prince Charles to Lady Diana Spencer.

A WONDERFUL LIFE

1981, a quarter century ago, was the year I entered the financial services business as a registered representative for a large national brokerage firm. The Dow was just around 1,000 and was just breaking out of a decade-long slump. I labored long and hard to build my client base, and I am proud today that many of the client relationships that began early in my career not only still exist, but have turned into cherished friendships. When I made my first "cold call" to my first prospective client (who hung up on me), I was a husband and father of two young daughters.

When I went to visit prospective clients twenty-five years ago, I had to park my orange Vega wagon around the corner and walk a block so as not to make a poor impression. I am grateful that, since then, enough people have placed their trust and confidence in me to allow me to support my family and upgrade my mode of transportation. My little family has since grown to include my phenomenal wife, Debby; my three beautiful daughters, Jenna (married to Ed), Cerissa (married to Brian), and Jael; my two sons,

Jonathon, Jr., and Jake; and my three—count 'em, three!—grandsons, Carson, Noah, and Landon. (That has since grown to eight grandchildren and counting.)

While I was building my business, we ate almost exclusively from our garden. Debby became a wizard at making zucchini, squash, and tomatoes look and taste different every night. I really did drive our bright orange Vega wagon to appointments and park around the corner so prospective clients would not see how poor I was. In reality, though, I was rich. I had a beautiful wife who believed in me and a growing family that we enjoyed, along with a God that was faithful.

After a few years of working two to three nights a week cold-calling and begging for business, I felt I could spare one night a week to go back to school and finish my MBA, which I did in 1986. We had a third daughter by then, and I attained my Certified Financial Planner designation at the same time. By 1989, I became disenchanted with the business model of the large investment firms (the wire houses) and joined Legg Mason, a regional brokerage firm. Three years later I left Legg Mason to join Janney Montgomery Scott, a regional firm based in Philadelphia. I believed then, and believe now, that the regional firm business model is better for me and my clients. These firms "manufacture" no products, and therefore there is no pressure to sell proprietary products or services. It allows me to be independent and serve my clients in the most effective way.

The investment business is tough and competitive and requires a special set of skills. You have to be able to make a recommendation with confidence and conviction, knowing that you could be dead wrong. Then you have to do it again, even if you were wrong the first time. Over time, if you are simply right more than you are wrong, then you will do well for your clients. Like Zig Ziglar used to say, "You can have anything in life you want, if you just help enough other people get what they want." That is what I set out to do and continue to do every day when I go to work. As I said before, it is harder than it looks. Building any business is hard work, and keeping it going and making it grow is even harder. I have worked very hard and also been very blessed to have met and been influenced by some truly wonderful people.

Lessons from Conrad

The first and most influential person in my life and later my business was my father, Conrad, a baker. He taught me many lessons growing up. Mostly, he taught by example, working long hours to build his business, provide for his family, send his kids to college, and eventually retire. I have tried to follow his lead as a loving father and husband and as a hardworking businessman. I watched how he loved and cherished my mother, how he cared for his parents when they grew older, and how he poured his life into others as a friend, father, Little League coach, and businessman. He was frequently the life of the party, and when he had money in his pocket, you wanted to be around him. He showed me a work ethic that I have tried to emulate throughout my life and career. Today in my practice, I apply some of his favorite phrases, which help me to keep perspective and stay focused.

"It's a jungle out there." To think that life and, more specifically, investing will be easy is naive at best. Accumulating, preserving, distributing, and transferring wealth is not easy and should be entered into with the expectation that there will be many obstacles along the way. A well thought-out plan is a must to overcome those obstacles. That is why I believe the advice and counsel of a qualified and dedicated financial professional is essential.

From the Summer 2004 newsletter:

GOOD APPROACH

It is time for my periodic baseball analogy. Jonathon, Jr. (then 18), and Jake (then 14) are both playing baseball at very competitive levels. Junior finished his senior season with a .500 batting average, broke the school RBI record, and tied the school record for career hits. Jake has come into his own this year and has been hitting the ball with authority. The pitchers they face throw hard, but they also throw curves, sliders, cutters, and knuckleballs. They have about one-half of one second to decide whether or not to swing. They do well because they have a good "approach." Investors can also increase their odds of success by having a good approach.

- *Have a plan.* A hitter needs to have a plan before stepping up to the plate. Depending upon what type of pitcher he is facing, how many outs, how many runners are on base, and even the score, the hitter's objective may differ. Does he want to be aggressive or "work the count"? Does he need to hit the ball deep or simply make contact? The investor also needs to adjust his or her objective depending upon life's circumstances. Do we want to be aggressive or preserve capital? Are we looking for long-term gains or current income? We need to have a plan.
- *See the ball.* In order to hit a baseball, you have to see it, recognize the pitch, and decide whether you can accomplish your goal by swinging at that pitch. An investor needs to also "see the ball" by knowing what he owns, and how the things he owns fit into

his plan. Rather than accumulating a series of "hot tips," the portfolio should be designed to fit into the investor's plan.

- *Don't chase.* Sometimes my sons will strike out by swinging at pitches in the dirt. They tell me later that the pitch looked "fat" until they swung and it curved, or dropped, or tailed away. Disciplined hitting requires that you keep your hands back as long as possible so you can recognize the pitch and avoid swinging at pitches that only look fat. A disciplined investor stays with investments that fit into his plan and avoids swinging at deals that look fat. Do not chase performance or go outside of your strike zone.
- *Go with the pitch.* A good hitter should be prepared to hit all types of pitches and adjust accordingly. The good investor should be prepared to include all types of sectors and asset classes in his or her portfolio and adjust accordingly. A roaring economy favors growth sectors, while a slowing economy favors defensive sectors. A well-diversified portfolio, rebalanced periodically, will increase an investor's odds for success.

An investor needs to have a plan based upon their life circumstances that takes into consideration all possible scenarios: inflation and rising interest rates, bull or bear markets, deflation and falling interest rates, and "Black Swan" events.

"More horsepower, less horse sense." Conrad used this one to let me know that driving too fast was not smart, or that "slow and steady wins the race." In the investing world, it is more prudent and the odds of success are much higher if we try to accumulate wealth slowly, rather than try to beat the market with hot stock picks. You need to have a process that is scalable, repeatable, and flexible. While the plan is very important, it is the execution that is critical. In order to hit a baseball you have to see it, recognize the pitch, and decide whether you can accomplish your goal by swinging at that pitch. An investor needs to also "see the ball" by knowing what he owns and how those things fit into his plan. Rather than accumulating a series of hot tips, or wild swings, the portfolio should be designed to fit the investor's plan.

From the Fall 1997 newsletter:

Good Form, Son

My son, Jonathon, became a long ball hitter this year in Little League with seven home runs and many more doubles and triples. While I like to think he takes after his good old dad, he reminds me more of his Uncle Mark, who could hit a ball so hard it was frightening. At only twelve years old, he is not big and strong, and his swing looks almost effortless. So, how does he do it? The answer is good form—a disciplined approach to swinging the bat which produces excellent bat speed and, so, power. Whenever he begins to think "home run" and abandons his discipline, he has problems. It sounds simple but is not that easy.

The goal for most investors should be minimizing their risks while optimizing their returns. "Good form" in attaining this goal is to invest systematically in a diverse mix of bonds and stocks of both large and small companies located both in the United States and around the world. Simple. The hard part is maintaining the original discipline by rebalancing the portfolio periodically—reducing the overperformers and adding to the underperformers.

Most people tend to do the opposite by selling the underperformers and adding to the overperformers—going for home runs.

That's why the best-selling funds this year are S&P Index funds (last year's best performers) while small- and mid-cap funds (last year's underperformers) are experiencing net redemptions. What is the result of this undisciplined, performance-chasing, short-term thinking and home run–swinging behavior? Since the end of May the S&P Mid-Cap 400 and Small-Cap 600 indices have each risen 15 percent, while the S&P 500 (a large-cap index) has risen only 9 percent. When the market corrected in late August, the mid-cap and small-cap indices were virtually flat, displaying strength in a negative market.

Those of you who have been rebalancing over the past few quarters—reducing large-cap positions and adding to small-cap positions—experienced much better results over the last quarter than the index-chasers.

Successful investing over a long period of time—the time it takes to meet your goals and objectives—requires discipline and good form.

From the Year-End 2003 newsletter:

The Secret to Success

I always remind my wonderful children that a few simple disciplines practiced every day are the key to a successful life. For example, if you want to be a better hitter, you need to swing a baseball bat every day. If you want to be a better point guard, you need to dribble a basketball every day. If you want to be a better student, you need to spend a little time every day in the library. If you want to be a better employee, you need to find a way to learn more about your company or job every day. All of these disciplines need to be practiced whether you feel like it or not.

If you want to be a better investor, you also need to practice a few simple disciplines every day, whether you feel like it or not. Such disciplines include diversification, asset allocation, rebalancing, and taking a long-term view even when the news is negative. Proper diversification using the principle of asset allocation will always result in something in your portfolio not working. Think about it—if everything was going up the same amount at the same time, then there would be no diversity and you would be exposed to the risk of everything going down at the same time. It is not easy to hold on to assets that are underperforming simply for diversification's sake.

Rebalancing a portfolio is an even more difficult discipline to adhere to. Selling some of your best-performing assets allows you to buy low and sell high systematically. However, it is hard to do! The temptation is to sell all of your "losers" and chase performance by adding to the winners. Hence the need for discipline—doing what you have to do, when you have to do it, whether you feel like it or not.

"It's nice to be important, but more important to be nice." My job is to help people meet their goals and objectives, and I could not do that effectively if I did not truly care. Personal, caring, loving service will help more than a long list of credentials. If I am successful in helping people, then my income will take care of itself.

From the Spring 2009 newsletter:

What Matters

I like to read the local paper, and last week I came across an open letter to the editor from a father named Marty thanking everybody for their prayers and support for his son Dave, who had just returned from a second stint in Iraq. It was accompanied by a picture of the whole family. The letter was heartfelt, and Marty was truly grateful for the support of the community and happy to have his son back home with him.

The last time I had been with Dave and his dad was five years ago. I was coaching the Senior League team from West Deptford in the Eastern Regional Tournament. We were the host district champs and were playing against the state champions from Maine to Maryland at our field. The other coaches and I wanted the experience to be special, so we took the team out to breakfast and lunch and acted like we were on the road. Dave was on the team, and Marty was with us at the meals.

When the subject of work came up, Marty informed us that his employer had given him an ultimatum to show up at work or be fired. He said that we would never get to experience something like this again, and, since we were spending it with our sons, he did not want to miss it—so he quit his job! Seeing the picture of Marty and Dave in the paper and knowing that Dave had risked his life to protect me and my family, I realized how right Marty had been. Some things are truly priceless and matter more than money.

This time last year Jon, Jr., was enjoying his last college baseball season. In April I traveled to Birmingham, Alabama, to watch him play in a weekend series. I was happy to be near my son, sharing the afternoon on a beautiful, sunny day. Junior was having a good series, but in the last game he struck out by watching three straight pitches go by. As was my habit, whenever he had a bad at-bat, I would change my seat. So I walked behind the dugout, where I came upon another father spending the afternoon with his son. They were enjoying the game and enjoying each other's company, happy to be sharing a beautiful afternoon. However, the father was pushing his son in a wheelchair. It was obvious that he had never been able to watch his son play in a game.

My son's strikeout at once became less important, and I realized how fortunate I was just to be spending time with him. After the game I hugged him extra tight as he got on the team bus. I was soon on a plane back to Philadelphia, returning to provide "caring financial management" to you. And while the financial management part is important, I believe it is the caring that truly matters.

"Be good to the people you meet on the way up, because you may meet the same people on the way down." This was one of my favorite sayings. It was my dad's way of telling me to never forget where I came from. If we appreciate and remember the discipline it took to attain everything worthwhile, we are more likely to keep growing professionally and personally. It is also important to remember all of the people who helped you along the way and thank them whenever you can. I incorporate this lesson by staying involved with local charities, organizations, and causes that are important to my family, my friends, and my clients.

From the Winter 2011 newsletter:

HOPE LIVES HERE

A few months ago I came home on a Thursday to find my grandson Carson in severe pain. There was a virus going around, and he seemed to have caught it. But after several hours his head hurt so badly he could hardly move. It was getting scary, so my daughter decided to take him to Children's Hospital of Philadelphia (CHOP). The next day, tests were being run and he was being kept as comfortable as possible. On Saturday I postponed my normal visit to the local gym and went to see my grandson, hoping for the best but still very concerned.

I was amazed at how nice and modern the hospital was and how many doctors were around. When I entered Carson's room, he was sitting on the side of his bed with a huge smile on his face and asking for food! I was happy and very relieved. He had been properly diagnosed with viral meningitis but was being treated and feeling better already, and the doctors and staff truly cared about his well-being. I told my kids that if anything ever happens to me, dress me up like a little kid and take me to CHOP!

I left and went to the gym, where I saw my friend Jeff. Jeff and his wife, Judy, had spent a great deal of time at CHOP with their son, Bryce. Bryce was born August 8, 2000, and diagnosed with a brain tumor on Father's Day 2002. He spent nine months receiving chemotherapy treatments at CHOP before passing away. Jeff and Judy have since set up Bryce's Bridge of Hope to raise funds through golf outings and other events, and to give other families hope that one day there will be better treatments and ultimately a cure for pediatric brain tumors. Every time I see Carson smile, I remember how lucky I am. I think of Jeff, Judy, and Bryce, and the hope they provide to others.

That is the reason I support Bryce's Bridge of Hope and will again be sponsoring the *Coaches vs. Cancer Tourney Tip-Off Breakfast* this year. More than six hundred basketball fans, business leaders, and corporate sponsors enjoy a morning of food and fun on the floor of the Palestra as local sports media panelists and the Philadelphia coaches compare their picks for the NCAA Tournament.

From the Winter 2014 newsletter:

HOPE LIVES HERE—STILL

Shortly after her first birthday party a week before Thanksgiving, my granddaughter, Ally, developed a stubborn virus. When she became extremely lethargic, she was taken to CHOP, where she was diagnosed as one of the youngest juvenile diabetics they have ever seen. Once again, I am amazed at the wonderful work being done at CHOP. Ally was sent home for Thanksgiving but returned for a few more days to stabilize her sugar levels and get the virus out of her. She is home now, and mommy Cerissa, daddy Brian, and frequent babysitter Mom-Mom Debby are testing her sugar regularly, monitoring her diet, and giving her insulin to keep her stable. She is doing well so far and is a happy baby. Pop-Pop loves when she gives him kisses. Please keep her in your thoughts and prayers. (Ally has since been fitted with an insulin pump and is doing well.)

Among the many organizations I support is Coaches vs. Cancer, a program founded by the American Cancer Society and the National

Association of Basketball Coaches that empowers coaches, their teams, and communities to make a difference in the fight against cancer. When I saw how much the organizers cared, it inspired me to get involved. In addition, as a result of Ally's condition, we have become involved with JDRF, the organization dedicated to funding Type 1 diabetes research. If I can make a small difference in someone else's life or be a blessing to someone each day, then that day has been worthwhile.

From the Summer 2007 newsletter:

Doing the Right Thing

It was a little over four years ago that thirteen-year-old Natalie Gilbert forgot the words to the National Anthem before an NBA playoff game. Former Sixers player and coach Maurice Cheeks, then the coach of the Portland Trailblazers, stepped in, offering a steady hand and a shaky voice in support. Cheeks saw a kid in need and reacted. The world saw a completely honest, unrehearsed act of simple human decency.

On Sunday, July 8 of this year, the Phillies showed the human decency and character that we used to hope our kids would learn from playing and watching sports. During a rain delay in Colorado, a gust of wind turned a routine covering of the infield into a scary situation. With several members of the Rockies ground crew in danger of being suffocated under the tarp, the Phillies rushed onto the field to help them get the tarp safely under control. Reigning National League MVP Ryan Howard used his home-run hitting strength to hold the tarp in place. Shane Victorino threw all of his body weight into dragging the tarp back. Jimmy Rollins was in the thick of it, and so was Adam

Eaton, the Phillies' starter that day. Abraham Nunez helped throw sandbags into place to secure the tarp. Even coach Jimmy Williams, who is sixty-three, helped out. At that moment, these world-class athletes were simply normal guys doing the right thing.

While I cannot guarantee investment results, I can promise to provide personal, caring service. Every recommendation may not work out, but it will be made with the best intentions. I continue to value the trust and confidence you have placed in me and will strive to earn it by consistently attempting to do the right thing.

I have had the pleasure of having friends as clients and clients become friends. What began in many cases as business became personal. I have been able to touch peoples' lives, and they have touched mine in so many ways. I am grateful that so many have entrusted me with such an important part of their lives.

I have shared in the joy of their children and grandchildren being born, and in the trials, tribulations, and triumphs of watching them grow up. I have suffered along with many through the extended illness or loss of a spouse and witnessed the anguish over long-term care decisions for loved ones. I have lost sleep worrying about their investments so they would not have to. I hope that I have made their lives better by taking some of the worry out of reaching their financial objectives. I resolve to stay armed with as much education, knowledge, and technology as possible, stay excited about the business I am in, and take advantage of every opportunity to improve.

CHAPTER TWO

Investor No-No's

I meet with individuals and families all the time. Their stories are all different, yet all the same. They all want to save and accumulate enough to send their kids to college, to upgrade their own lifestyles, and to reach a certain age where they can make work optional. However, according to a recent study by Bankrate.com, a full third of people in the richest country in the world have nothing saved for retirement. The obstacles to saving enough are similar ... the kids' college took priority, or an aging parent needed more help than anticipated. Basically, life gets in the way. Worse still, most well-intentioned Americans do not have the time, temperament, or training to manage long-term investments. It's not their fault—they're human. And that's why they hire professionals.

From the Summer 2014 newsletter:

PERFORMANCE ANXIETY

DALBAR, Inc., is the financial community's leading independent expert for evaluating, auditing, and rating business practices, customer performance, product quality, and service. Launched in 1976, DALBAR has earned recognition for consistent and unbiased evaluations of investment companies and investment professionals. Since 1994, DALBAR's Quantitative Analysis of Investor Behavior (QAIB) has been measuring the effects of investor decisions to buy, sell, and switch into and out of mutual funds over both the short and long term. The results consistently show that the average investor earns less—in many cases, much less—than mutual fund performance reports would suggest (DALBAR, 2014). The problem, according to DALBAR, is investor behavior.

Meanwhile, according to Vanguard, the value of working with an advisor is peace of mind and is very real. Working with an advisor can add "about 3 percent" in net returns when following the Vanguard Advisor's Alpha framework for wealth management, particularly for taxable investors. "Some of the most significant opportunities to add value occur during periods of market duress or euphoria, when clients are tempted to abandon their well-thought-out investment plan" (Vanguard, *"Putting a Value on Your Value: Quantifying Vanguard Advisor's Alpha,"* March 2014). My conclusion is that a well-thought-out and implemented plan with the help and guidance of a qualified, caring financial professional gives one the best chance to meet financial goals and be in a position to make work optional.

I have found that the most basic mistakes—or No-No's—are the same for everyone and correspond to the basic "Lessons from Conrad."

NO PLAN

Proverbs 29:18 says that "where there is no vision, the people perish." Put another way, if we have no idea where we are going, we probably will not be happy when we get there. When people "try" investing by "taking a flyer" with no idea what they are looking to achieve, they are on a path to nowhere. *The Seven Habits of Highly Effective People,* first published in 1989, is a business and self-help book written by Stephen R. Covey. It has sold more than 15 million copies in thirty-eight languages worldwide, and the audio version has sold 1.5 million copies. It remains one of the best-selling nonfiction business books. Covey presents an approach to being effective in attaining goals by aligning oneself to what he calls "true north" principles of a character ethic that he presents as universal and timeless. In August 2011, *Time* listed *Seven Habits* as one of the "25 Most Influential Business Management Books."

Habit number two in Covey's book is "begin with the end in mind." When we begin with the end in mind, we have a personal direction to guide our daily activities, without which we will accomplish little toward our own goals. It's part of controlling our own lives. All things are created twice; first in our minds, and then we work to bring them into physical existence. By taking control of our own first creation, we can write or rewrite our own scripts, thus taking some control and responsibility for the outcome.

The worst plan is "beating the market." First of all, what market? If you mean the S&P 500 (which is what most people think), how would you like to have beaten the market from 2000 to 2010 by, say, one percent per year? Congratulations! If you started with a nest egg of $1,000,000 and took out $50,000 per year to live, you just turned your nest egg into $621,347 instead of only $540,774 (the "market" return). And guess what? If you had no plan and no process (as discussed in the following pages) you probably would have given up midway through the decade! Timing is *not* everything—planning is.

From the Winter 2001 newsletter:

SUPER UPSET

In case you missed it, the sports world recently witnessed one of the greatest upsets since Joe Namath's Jets defeated the mighty Baltimore Colts in Super Bowl III. The hands-down favorite was described afterward as "a bit distracted." For the winner, "every step was right." The action was riveting as Surrey Spice Girl became the first miniature poodle to win the prestigious Westminster Dog Show since 1959. The three-year-old upset heavy favorite Torum's Scarf Michael, a Kerry blue terrier. Kaz Hosaka expertly led Spice around the center ring and could hardly talk after the victory. "I came to this country twenty-three years ago hoping to win this show," he said. Only in America can dreams like that come true!

Speaking of upsets, this year's Super Bowl also produced a shocker, as the heavily favored St. Louis Rams lost to the New England Patriots. It is appropriate that a team called the Patriots, with colors of red, white, and blue, win one of sports' biggest prizes during this time in our nation's history. However, not many people predicted that they could beat "the greatest show on turf." Almost man for man, the Rams were bigger, faster, and more talented. Oddsmakers had them as sixteen-point favorites. So how did the Patriots win? They had a better game plan and they played as a team.

Plan to Win

As the Patriots showed, a superior plan is more important than having superior players. Likewise, a well-thought-out and rigorously followed investment plan can overcome poor market timing and shoddy stock selection. Many studies have concluded that asset allocation is the single greatest determinant of investment performance—not market timing or stock selection. That's why an investment plan is so important. This plan should include:

- a summary of an investor's financial goals (why are you investing?);
- nominal return benchmarks (8 percent, 10 percent, 12 percent?);
- a definition of risk and risk tolerance (how much can you stand?);
- a time frame for review and evaluation (quarterly, annually?);
- an asset allocation policy (what combination of asset classes could maximize returns with minimum risk?);
- a procedure for selecting, buying, and selling instruments, funds, or money managers;
- income and cash flow needs (how much and when?).

NO PROCESS

When we set out on a journey, in this case a journey to financial freedom, we cannot become sidetracked with every distraction. Proverbs 4:25–27 instructs us: "Let your eyes look directly ahead, and let your gaze be fixed straight in front of you. Watch the path of your feet, and all of your ways will be established. Do not turn to the right nor to the left." Distractions can be "shiny objects on the beach," such as TV commercials touting gold and silver coins, talking heads posing as experts while seeking to merely entertain, hot tips from your uncle (or barber or neighbor), frightening headlines in the news, or any other event that knocks you off course. If you have a process to deal with all of this and stick to it, you give yourself a chance. A few simple disciplines practiced every day—doing what no one else is willing to do until you can do what no one else is able to do—is the way to financial freedom. Accumulating hot tips has very low odds of success.

From the Winter 2003 newsletter:

Battle-Tested Theory

The overall plan devised to defeat an enemy is called strategy. The actual techniques carried out against the enemy are tactics. Once the overall strategic plan has been approved, planning cycles at lower echelons are implemented. Offensive actions involve operations that will force the defeat of armed forces and destroy an enemy's will to fight. Defense entails the employment of all means and methods to prevent, resist, or destroy an enemy attack. Its purpose may be twofold: to gain time pending the development of more favorable conditions to take the offensive, or to concentrate forces in one area for decisive offense elsewhere.

Modern Portfolio Theory

The lessons of war can be applied to investing. The overall investment plan devised to reach your goal is called the Strategic Asset Allocation. Once the overall strategic plan has been approved, Tactical Asset Allocation attempts to further improve portfolio performance by making ongoing adjustments—tactics—within the overall strategy in response to short-term changes in the markets and economy. Offensive actions or tactics involve investing in momentum and growth while the markets and economy are accelerating. Defensive tactics entail the employment of all means to preserve capital while the markets are retreating to gain time pending the development of more favorable conditions.

Proper asset allocation involves the combination of asset classes that have a low or negative correlation. An example of items with low correlation would be skis and bicycles. Skis would be useful during a snowstorm, while a bicycle would have greater value on a sunny day. To enjoy yourself over a long period of time, you need to have both, but you can only use and enjoy one at a time. Investing examples would be small company growth stocks and short-term Treasury bonds. The former can generate very high returns during sunny days—when the economy is humming and optimism abounds. During snowstorms—when the outlook is dreary and uncertain—Treasuries will preserve capital and provide minimal returns. Over long periods of time, you need to have both asset classes in your portfolio to prosper, but only one at a time is working. That is the main characteristic of a properly diversified portfolio: at any given point in time something in your portfolio should not be working. If everything is working, you are going to suffer when the investment climate changes. This lesson in common sense earned Harry Markowitz a Nobel Prize in Economics when he called it Modern Portfolio Theory.

From the Winter 2009 newsletter:

Short-Term Adjustments to the Long-Term Plan

In the bubbly euphoria of the home clubhouse after the Phillies captured their first championship in twenty-eight years, Jamie Moyer reeled off a list of people who made it happen.

He spoke of the way the Phillies had played with purpose all season. Holding them together, Moyer said, was Manager Charlie Manuel. "Charlie's been huge to this club," Moyer said. "He's just got this air about him that everything's okay. He gets respect from the players."

Manuel, 64, has been belittled for his ill-fitting uniform, his avuncular nature, his unusual syntax. But he outfoxed everybody this season, making the right moves in the Game 5 clincher while his counterpart, Joe Maddon of the Rays, seemed to make the wrong ones (The New York Times 10/31/08).

Charlie was successful because he stuck to his basic long-term plan, while making minor adjustments and daily moves—some of which worked and some did not. But over time the plan worked, and we all celebrated. The same is true of our investment plans. Things do not always go as planned in the short term, and every adjustment and short-term move does not always work. The key is to have a well-thought-out, comprehensive long-term plan which every short-term adjustment should support. The biggest mistake we can make is to jump on and off the bandwagon—that can really hurt our chances for long-term success.

From the Summer 1997 newsletter:

But Remember

Be good to the people you meet on the way up because you meet the same people on the way down. The run-up in stock values has shifted many investors' allocations so that a total portfolio may no longer be properly diversified. As the market value of the most aggressive (and risky) parts of a portfolio increases, the percentage of assets devoted to these risky assets also rises. The result is increased exposure to stock market risk and a portfolio that's out of balance relative to your original objectives and risk tolerance.

Crash Test Dummy

When your portfolio is out of balance, especially when overweighted in stocks or funds that have gone way up, you should take a look at how that might affect your portfolio in a serious market decline or crash. Even if it were a temporary decline, you should at least know what to expect.

NO IDEA

If you do not care about anything, then anything will do. If you care a little, you might have a little chance for success. But if you care enough, you can achieve great things. You cannot "dabble" with investments and build a portfolio that creates great wealth over time. Many people only care about their investments when they hear or read about how the markets are going up or have hit new highs (greed), or when they hear or read about how the markets are crashing and heading lower (fear). In order to be effective in building, preserving, and distributing wealth, you have to care all of the time and care enough to engage in the process continuously. As my high school history teacher and football coach used to say, "Everything counts."

Unfortunately, financial plans and investment portfolios do not run by themselves. They need to be reviewed, managed, and updated periodically to reflect both changing market conditions and changes in life circumstances. I cannot tell you how many unreturned phone calls I make because people simply do not want to be bothered. It might sound ridiculous, but it is true. It is also true that many times people resist making any updates or changes because they do not want to incur any expenses. I will address that later, but suffice it to say that being penny-wise and pound-foolish when it comes to one's investments can have dramatic negative effects over time.

From the Winter 1999 newsletter:

Everything Counts

By only focusing on your investments, you're only seeing part of the picture. There is an entire spectrum of lifestyle issues spanning all generations of your family. A comprehensive financial planning overview can help you answer these questions:

- Are my assets positioned to minimize taxes?
- Are my investments working in concert with my estate plans?
- Is there some way to put the built-up cash value of my insurance to better use?
- Now that my mortgage is paid off, does my insurance picture change at all?
- I'm changing jobs. What do I do with my 401(k)?

- What do I need to know about my pension before retiring?
- Should I take a lump-sum distribution or a monthly pension?
- Who will make financial decisions if I become incapacitated?
- Should I have a will, an estate plan?
- When I die, is there a way to ensure my children don't get too much money all at once?
- Should I be preparing now for the possibility of a nursing home someday?

The above questions need to be answered as part of an effective financial plan. They cannot be ignored before it is too late.

NO PURPOSE

It would be easy to say that the only purpose for investing is to make money. But there must be a deeper purpose if you are going to take the time to plan, make the effort to stick with a process, and care enough to pay attention to the changing economic landscape and your changing life circumstances. Your reasons for investing are bound to change as you go through the ups and downs of life. This is an important process, because the only other option is to invest with no purpose, which will likely result in investing practices that reflect your uncertainty and cause your returns to suffer.

Your reasons and goals will have to be reviewed and adjusted as your circumstances change. Even if nothing significant has changed, it is always helpful to reacquaint yourself with your reasons at regular intervals to see how you have progressed. At the end of one of my favorite movies, *Vision Quest,* the lead character, Louden Swain, played by Matthew Modine, sums things up by saying: "But all I ever settled for is that we're born to live and then to die, and ... we got to do it alone, each in his own way. And I guess that's why we got to love those people who deserve it like there's no tomorrow. 'Cause when you get right down to it, there isn't." Your investments should be another way to "love those people who deserve it" by building a financial wall around your family and others that you care about. If you accumulate enough wealth, you can have a positive effect on people and causes well beyond your family and friends.

From the Spring 2000 newsletter:

BELIEVE IN YOURSELF

A leading online broker implies that if you "believe in yourself" and use your instincts, you can "beat the market." I can't make market-beating promises. I can only promise personal, caring service while providing customized solutions to help you meet your unique financial objectives. My goal is to help you relax and enjoy life and allow you to focus on what you enjoy and do best.

If you really believe in yourself, then you don't need to beat the market to be happy. Lifestyle is what it's all about, not merely achieving wealth. What you do with your life is what matters. Wealth can be a tool for achieving the freedom to maximizing your experience and your impact on others. I appreciate the opportunity to be part of that.

From the Summer 2000 newsletter:

LEAVE YOUR MARK

Nuveen Investments offers products to help investors build and sustain wealth. Their motto is: Invest well. Look ahead. Leave your mark. They claim that "our investments provide us with tremendous power to make positive things happen" and ask, "How will you make a difference? How will you leave your mark?"

A teenager from Boston began investing at the age of fifteen, using money he received at his bar mitzvah. He parlayed his investments into a respectable sum, which he could have used to indulge in whatever teenage fantasy he desired. He decided this year to "make a difference" by honoring his childhood friend who had died of leukemia at age six. To honor his friend's memory, he has endowed a $1,000 college scholarship for someone who understands "that people should give more than they take."

From the Fall 2001 newsletter, following the 9/11 terrorist attacks:

BIG HAT, NO CATTLE

Many people confuse expensive cars, watches, and suits with wealth. Even Webster's Dictionary defines wealth as "an abundance of material possessions." At my college graduation party many years ago, my father defined wealth in terms I will never forget. The party included friends and relatives that I normally only saw at weddings and funerals. As he looked over the group celebrating and enjoying each other's company, he said, "We're millionaires already, and we don't even know it." How true.

One of the positive results of recent events has been the renewed emphasis on that which is truly important and valuable. We cherish our freedom more. We appreciate our families and friends and neighbors more and hug our children more. We are reevaluating our priorities and adjusting our lifestyles to reflect what is most important.

I have found, quite simply, that if I can help people avoid these basic No-No's, then I can have an immeasurable affect on their financial life. That is not as easy as it sounds. As I said before, investors are human. In the next chapter I explain some of the most common and potentially harmful mistakes people make and how to avoid them.

CHAPTER THREE

Mistakes to Avoid at All Costs

Greatness is the result of a lot of little things done well over and over again. If that is true, then mediocrity is the result of a lot of little things done poorly over and over again. Below I look at some of the same mistakes I see being made over and over, regardless of the market environment.

MISTAKE #1: GREAT EXPECTATIONS

I have heard people say that you should never invest money that you cannot afford to lose. However, that is a bit extreme and may scare people away from investing at all. What you should do is avoid making your first investment with unrealistic expectations. In other words, do not start out treating investments like the lottery or the stock market like a casino. Begin with a diversified portfolio, like a mutual fund or unit investment trust, and use money that you can afford to part with for a long time. Give your investments and yourself a chance to make money by taking a long-term view.

Anticipate that the investment can, in fact, lose value temporarily, and be prepared to add money systematically.

Many people begin their investing experience under false pretenses. They hear about something on TV or get a "tip" from a friend or neighbor, or read an article. They think they have information ahead of the rest of the world and can get in on the ground floor of an amazing opportunity and make a lot of money in a short period of time.

Sound investing requires an understanding of what exactly a share of stock is. A share of stock is not a lottery ticket! It represents an ownership position in a company and entitles the owner to participate in the success or failure of that company. That success or failure depends on the product or service that the company sells, the management of the company, and the vagaries of the marketplace. When a company is successful, the shares may entitle you to receive a dividend, which you can keep and spend or reinvest into additional shares of the company. One vagary that is difficult to understand is what makes a share of stock worth more or less in the future. This is where risk comes into play. That is why it is prudent to invest in more than one company and invest systematically over a long period of time.

One of the worst things that can happen is that you treat the markets like a casino and are right the first time. This leads many to believe they are a lot smarter than they are. It is also a mistake to believe that you will be different than others when it comes to emotional behavior. Thinking that you will not succumb to fear and greed at the wrong times is dangerous. You should establish your investment plan in a vacuum.

I have noticed that people's tolerance for risk changes with the market. When the market is up, people will think they want to take on more risk. What they are really saying is that they are willing to take more risk as long as the market keeps going up! Before you invest, expect the markets to fluctuate and have a plan to deal with those fluctuations.

From the Winter 2011 newsletter:

> ### GREAT EXPECTATIONS
>
> Here in Philadelphia we love our sports heroes, including Eagles Ron Jaworski, Wilbert Montgomery, and Harold Carmichael. As a matter of fact, their teammate, Bill Bergey, will be honored this year by the Philadelphia Sports Writers Association as a Living Legend (Philadelphia Inquirer, Jan. 15, 2011). Those same sports writers ran Donovan McNabb out of town last year.
>
> What does Donovan McNabb have in common with living legend Bill Bergey and his teammates? They both went to the Super Bowl and they both lost! What separates them? The current version of the Eagles—called the Gold Standard by owner Jeffrey Laurie—has been expected to win it all every year, while Bergey's 1980 team was not. Apparently, the results are not what makes a success or failure, but whether or not those results meet expectations.
>
> The headline recently in the Philadelphia Inquirer said, "In 2010, Most Made a Bundle" (Jan. 16, 2011). The article claims, "In 2010, it was almost impossible to make a mistake" unless you decided to "play it safe with cash or CDs" or "cling to Treasury Bonds." I submit that at mid-year, not many people expected the stock market to beat its historical averages like it did. It was easy to be spooked by the "flash crash" and subsequent 16 percent plunge in stocks in the summer and play it safe. That is why so many were pulling money out of

stock funds and putting money into bond funds during the year. (See: *Mutual Investors Prefer Bonds*, Investorplace.com, September 13, 2010). It was very possible to make a mistake last year by getting caught up in short-term expectations and abandoning your long-term plan.

Another unrealistic expectation is the ability to beat the market. You cannot and should not expect to do so consistently over a long period of time. Anyone who tells you that they can is a liar or a fool or both, and should be ignored. The next best thing would be to equal the market by investing in an index that mirrors the return of the whole market. This may work for certain investors, but it has many pitfalls that I will talk about later.

From the Spring 1998 newsletter:

> ### BEARDSTOWN BLUNDER
>
> The Beardstown Ladies, a group of grandmotherly investors, achieved national fame for supposedly producing astounding returns on their portfolio. They sold 800,000 copies of a book touting annual returns of twice the market for the ten years through 1993, published four other books, and have spoken nationwide about their investment success.
>
> A long-unnoticed disclaimer on the copyright page of *The Beardstown Ladies' Common-Sense Investment Guide* says that the annual return covered in the book "includes the dues that the members pay regularly." Say what? When a Chicago magazine published an article questioning the returns claimed in the book, the Ladies submitted their results to an audit.
>
> Alas, their investment formula had produced results well below the market averages. It seems the "Beardstown

Blunder" was caused by an incorrect computer entry. But what about the buyers of the million-plus books offering a formula for ultra-safe investing with whopping returns? Oh, sorry, but that type of investment program does not exist! What the Beardstown Ladies' experience proves is that to achieve high returns, you need to assume a high level of risk.

Expectations of quick riches or a shortcut to wealth will ultimately, if not immediately, lead to disappointment. I recommend you diversify and manage the risks of investing with the goal of meeting your "family benchmark"—the return sufficient to meet the needs of you and your family to accomplish the goals you set out in your investment plan. Sticking to an investment process will keep you in the game during difficult markets and prevent you from getting sloppy or overly aggressive during good markets. This is a lot more difficult than it sounds, and like they say on TV, you should not try this at home! That is why I believe you should not expect to effectively manage your investment portfolio with the skill and discipline necessary to effectively meet you and your family's financial goals without the guidance of a competent, caring financial professional.

From the Spring 1998 newsletter:

> ### Danger
>
> The soaring stock market is tempting many investors to blindly assume a level of risk that, if they really thought about it, they would normally find foolish. How about this grandmotherly advice: An ounce of prevention is worth a pound of cure. How can you prevent having a portfolio that is not suited to your risk tolerance before it is too late?
>
> The "Investment Policy Statement" is a written statement that helps take some of the emotion out of investing.

A well-constructed investment policy statement should help keep your investments consistent with your risk tolerance.

From the Winter 1999 newsletter:

I Dream of Jeannie

Often people daydream about the riches and rewards that would be theirs if they only had a good crystal ball (or genie). Well, if you put yourself back a year ago and you had correctly forecast that the President would be impeached, but that prior to that Newt Gingrich would resign and his apparent successor, Bob Livingston, would resign before officially assuming the Speaker's duties; that Russia would default; that a major hedge fund would require a bailout by major banks and the Fed, that half the S&P Index and NASDAQ stocks would be down for the year, and overall corporate earnings would come in well below analysts' estimates ... you would have had a pretty good forecasting year. But should that have changed your investment plan? I hope not! Because, given that information, who would have guessed that the market averages would have gone up? That's why your investment plan should not be based on short-term events (even if you can predict them), but on your long-term goals and objectives.

From the Spring 2001 newsletter:

How Bad Will It Get?

On December 9, 1974, the cover of Time said "Recession's Greetings" and showed a torn and tattered Santa Claus. Shortly after that, the stock market went straight up—over 60 percent the next two years. On October 11, 1990, the cover of Time, referring to the stock market, read "High Anxiety." The Dow never went any lower, and a year later it was 25 percent higher. In March of 1996, the cover of US News & World Report showed a bull reading the stock pages with the caption, "The Aging Bull Market—Investor Beware!" The next twelve months saw another 25 percent rise in the Dow. September 1998 saw a number of negative headlines, including the Fortune cover story, "The Crash of '98: Can the US Economy Hold Up?" Today the Dow, even after the recent swoon, is about 25 percent higher.

Well, How Bad?

Over the past several weeks, every major magazine has come out with a bear market cover story, including the Business Week headline, "How Bad Will It Get?"

Well, I don't know. What I do know is that if you had invested $10,000 in the Dow each time a magazine announced a bear market on the covers cited above, your $40,000 investment would be worth over $230,000. Unfortunately, instead of investing, investors (or were they speculators?) yanked a reported $11.4 billion from stock mutual funds in February. Similar activity was recorded during the market lows of 1987, 1990, and 1998, which, in hindsight, were tremendous opportunities to buy, not sell.

One More Thing

I also know another thing. In 1960, when most of the people retiring today bought their first homes, the average new home cost $30,000. Today the average new home costs $140,000. Meanwhile, $30,000 in the S&P 500 would have grown to well over $600,000. That represents a profit five times greater than the investment most people think of as the best of their lifetime. So, treat your investment plan like you treat your home purchase to maximize your chances of success:

- Buy when you're afraid;
- Think long-term and ignore short-term noise;
- Keep adding money in good times and bad;
- Periodically review, monitor, and rebalance to add value; and
- Seek professional guidance.

From the Summer 2001 newsletter:

THE MANY LOVES OF DOBIE GILLIS

The coolest cat in the history of primetime TV, Maynard G. Krebs, was the beatnik friend of Dobie Gillis. Maynard lived in his own world with its own twisted logic. The "G" stood for Walter. Maynard was named after his Aunt Walter and Uncle Edith. His speech was full of colorful phrases, such as "You rang?" and "Like, I'm getting all misty." But Maynard G. Krebs will always be best remembered for his response whenever anyone mentioned the subject of work. He would instantaneously shudder and let out a plaintive cry of "Work?!"

OUT OF ORDER

Remember the truck driver who made so much money trading online that he bought an island? He had to sell it to meet his margin calls. The teenager with the helicopter? It was repossessed when his easy online profits disappeared. And Stuart? He was fired by Mr. B., who lost plenty taking his advice. These folks found out this truth: "The elevator to success is out of order. You must take the steps."

That brings me back to my original subject: work. Investing is not a get-rich-quick scheme. It is part of the financial planning process that helps us meet our financial goals and objectives over time, with hard work and discipline. We must follow the steps.

From the Spring 2000 newsletter, in an effort to encourage diversification before the tech bubble:

CHEF OF THE FUTURE

I remember when a 10 percent return made investors happy. To make money required careful analysis to uncover value. We looked for high dividends, low price-to-earnings, sound management, and a business that we could understand. This has been replaced by the "new paradigm, new economy" style in which we ride the latest fad and invest in themes, such as:

- voice over internet protocol;
- pixel-based 2-D animators;
- E-business application support platforms;
- orthodogonal frequency division multiplexing;
- dense wavelength division multiflexer optical fibers; and
- happy housewife handy helper.

Okay, the last one is for all of my fellow Honeymooners fans. While it may prove profitable to participate in the above technologies, don't forget the "fridge and medicine chest" stocks. People will still eat, shave, get headaches, and buy clothes, even in the new economy. And, as an added bonus, many of these companies have dividends, earnings, low P/E ratios, sound management, and businesses that we can understand. (But can it core "a" apple?)

From the Summer 2013 newsletter:

> ### The Family Benchmark
>
> For many, it is fun and interesting to talk about the market. I see people watching CNBC and Cramer every night while I am on the treadmill at the gym (keeping my promise to you to exercise and maintain a proper diet so I can stay alert and healthy to put in the time and effort necessary—see the "Lessons from Conrad" tab on the Leise Wealth Management Group website). He is very entertaining and often informative. But "beating the market" or trying to "pick winners" is not my goal and should not be yours. My job is to help you plan for and achieve your family benchmark—the return necessary to meet your long-term desires for you and your family, consistent with the risk you are willing to take. My team and I try to help you meet that benchmark while minimizing volatility and maximizing the certainty that you will be able to live the life you desire while providing personal, caring service to make the experience as stress-free as possible.

It is tempting to get caught up in the daily ups and downs of the economy and markets. Investing is hard work and requires discipline to stick within the parameters of a plan that was thought out to meet our objectives and yours alone.

MISTAKE #2: FIGHTING THE LAST WAR

Worse than being overly optimistic is having expectations shaped only by recent events, rather than by long-term historical evidence. This is often referred to as "investing in the rear-view mirror." In the previous example, the investors were pulling out of stock funds while stocks were going up. They were looking back instead of looking forward when making their investment decisions. Instead of continuing to invest systematically, confident that the averages would eventually return to the mean established over many decades of results, they extrapolated the declines of the prior few months. They were still fighting the last war.

Following the high inflation of the 1970s, most people were more interested in gold, natural resources, and oil going to $200 per barrel than finding the value in equities that existed. When interest rates were at ridiculously high rates in the early 1980s, most people chose the safety of high-yielding short-term money market funds rather than taking advantage of tremendous opportunities to lock in those yields for the long term in bonds or dividend-paying stocks. Leading up to the tech bubble, I was often challenged as to why I still recommended the "fridge and medicine cabinet" stocks of stable companies that were not participating in the technology boom. Then, when the bubble burst, it became difficult to get people to look at traditional technology companies that were actually earning money and paying dividends. Following the Great Recession and stock market decline of 2008, people are flocking to something called "crash-proof retirement" programs while the markets are recovering those losses and achieving new highs.

As of this writing, according to mutual fund flow statistics, investors are still reluctant to add to stock funds. In fact, they have been wary of stock funds since the current bull market began in March 2009. According to the Investment Company Institute, the funds' trade group, investors have yanked a net $86 billion from all stock funds and nearly $400 billion from US stock funds since the bull market run began (*2014 Investment Company Fact Book*). During that time, the major stock averages have appreciated well over 100 percent. The last war should not be forgotten, but it need not be fought again.

From the Fall 2010 newsletter:

Eternal Sunshine of the Spotless Mind

In the above-titled 2004 movie, Joel Barish (Jim Carrey) is an emotionally withdrawn man and Clementine Kruczynski (Kate Winslet) is his girlfriend and a dysfunctional free spirit. They are inexplicably attracted to each other despite their different personalities. They do not realize it at the time, but they are former lovers now separated after two years together. After a nasty fight, Clementine had her memories of their relationship erased from her mind. Upon learning this, Joel was devastated and went to have the same procedure done. But as Joel's memories progressively disappeared, he began to rediscover their earlier passion. When they learn later what was done, they realize that even if everything in life is not perfect, their relationship can still be worthwhile.

(The following refers to the 2008–09 financial crisis and market decline.) Investors are increasingly trying to erase bad memories of market volatility from their minds. According to a recent AP-CNBC poll of investors, 61 percent said the market's recent volatility has made them less confident about buying and selling stocks. And the majority of those surveyed—55 percent—said the market is fair only to some investors. This sentiment is supported by the fact that, from January 2008 through July of this year, investors have pulled a net $244 billion out of stock mutual funds (Associated Press, Alan Zibel, Sept. 14, 2010).

This is like someone who has had an auto accident vowing never to drive again. It may prevent them from being involved in another accident, but it makes it much more difficult to get where they need to go. Avoiding equities may prevent short-term pain, but it may hamper your ability to meet your long-term goals and objectives. Just like in the movie, even if the markets are not perfect, a long-term investment plan that includes equities can still be worthwhile.

From the Summer 2009 newsletter:

PICKING UP THE PIECES

No one expects investors who have lived through the past eighteen months to simply shrug it off and enthusiastically resume investing with the same expectations of ever-rising wealth. In the aftermath of the worst financial storm since the Great Depression, investors will need to understand that while past performance was no guarantee of future results in good times, the same holds true in bad. Do not make the mistake of relying too heavily on what happened in the recent past when it comes to predicting the future. Unless you already have all the money you need to fund your retirement, you still need to be invested to grow your portfolio and reach your goals.

Investing in the stock market from this point forward is a serious and necessary exercise that, like it or not, most investors need to participate in. In the new reality, you may not like the stock market. But these days, when defined benefits and other forms of entitlement plans are no longer a reliable part of the retirement equation, it's the reality in which we live. Investing for retirement is best viewed as a means to an end, a long-term program with the goal of replacing your income after you have stopped working. There's little room for the feelings that can sometimes derail you from that long-term objective.

From the Summer 1998 newsletter:

WEIJI

The Chinese use the same word for "crisis" and "opportunity." That Mandarin word—weiji—can be applied to today's stock market. The market's problems have by now been well documented:

- Asia, Japan and Russia
- Slowing economy
- Lowered earnings expectations
- Politics/Clinton's woes
- Y2K costs

While these problems have existed and been discussed since last fall (1997), they only now seem to have caught many off-guard. One well-known market strategist was calling for Dow 10,000 on a Monday, then changed to calling for Dow 7,600 on Tuesday after a 200-point drop. The problems that he cited on Tuesday were the same problems that existed on Monday. The only difference was that the market had dropped.

THE EXPECTED CORRECTED

A market "correction" denotes that something was wrong that needed to be fixed. While all of the problems noted above do exist, what really needed correcting was investor expectations. Many investors have come to expect the market to provide returns well above historical norms forever. Stocks are driven by future expectations. Now that the expectations for earnings and economic growth for the next six months have been lowered—corrected to reflect reality—stock prices have been lowered, as well.

Looking Ahead

The Great One (Wayne Gretzky) says that he is one of the greatest hockey players of all time because he always skates to where the puck is going to be. Many of the factors that had been driving the market higher are still in place today:

- Low inflation from global competition,
- Unprecedented productivity through technology and corporate consolidation, and
- The continued baby boom spending wave—the key driver of the economy for the next ten years.

To position yourself advantageously for the next ten years, you must invest demographically—that is, determine where the boomers are going next, and get there before them. If you have funds available, you should buy during corrections in those areas that will benefit as the baby boomers age.

Following the "Asian Contagion" and steep drop in the summer of 1998, I wrote a special edition to put the negative sentiment of the time into perspective and encourage investors to look beyond that sentiment. From the Special Edition 1998 newsletter:

Shattered

Is it safe yet? Well, the truth is, it never really was safe. We all forgot that the price we pay for high stock market returns is a high level of risk. For a while we were getting only the returns. Now we are getting the risk. It isn't fun, but for stock market investors, it is the price of doing business.

How bad is it? The S&P 500 is now down about 20 percent from its high, but that only represents the largest companies. The flight to liquidity has allowed the indexes to mask the bloodshed. The average NYSE and NASDAQ stock is now down more than 40 percent from its fifty-two-week high, with one-third of the universe down 50 percent or more. This broad-based deterioration is similar to that of the 1987 crash.

What now? The sort of decline we are experiencing has happened before, and it will happen again. According to Ibbotson Associates, there have been twenty-two declines of 10 percent since 1925, roughly equal to one every three and a half years. Half of those downturns turned into 20 percent declines.

Historically, the stock market has tended to take a substantial correction into the midterm elections (like this year).

Here's the good news: The gains in the market from the correction year–low to the high in the year following such four-year cycles has averaged 50 percent!

This suggests that the next strong overall stock market surge is likely to occur soon as data from the economy and profit picture eventually restore investor confidence. The major risk now would be to miss the rebound rather than to suffer through the rest of the correction.

Catch the Wave

Just like the crash of 1987 caused many to wonder if stocks would ever go up again, this market decline has people worried that the bull run is over. However, the run up which took the Dow from under 4,000 in late 1994 to over 9,000 recently follows the rampant debt-and-depression psychology of the early 1990s. Remember the S&L crisis, junk bond meltdown, the Latin America crisis, and "no new taxes" recession that made us get rid of George Bush in favor of Bill Clinton? Things were bad, yet we were on the brink of a huge bull market wave! We could be on the brink of another such wave. This wave is the result of another—the baby boom spending wave.

I followed up on the special edition with a message of encouragement, to look forward rather than in the rearview mirror. From the Fall 1998 newsletter:

Turn, Turn, Turn

"To everything there is a season, and a time to every purpose under heaven." The best time to buy stocks, according to Sir John Templeton, is when you have the money. Likewise, the best time to sell stocks is when you need the money. Some may feel it is better to buy when prices are low and sell when prices are high. The first time I ever saw my wife lose control of herself was early in our marriage, when we came upon a store with Cranberry glass at 50 percent off. She went nuts, and it almost scared me. Yet, when it comes to stocks, a "sale" is not viewed as an opportunity to buy value, but as a time to panic and question the value.

I am precluded from making any guarantees, but I can relate historical observations. So far, the long-term advance has been permanent, while the short-term declines have been temporary. Often, fear of the short-term replaces long-term opportunity. According to Lipper Analytical Services, investors pulled as much as $9 billion from stock funds in August. The last time the fund industry experienced net redemptions was September 1990—when, just like this year, the Dow had dropped 20 percent from its summer high and recession fear and the S&L crisis were in the headlines. On October 11, 1990, the Dow reached a low of 2,365. The cover of Time magazine that week proclaimed "High Anxiety." Within six months, the Dow had recovered <u>all</u> of the decline and went on to finish 1991 at 3,168—33 percent higher than when the net redemptions (sales) took place. Of course now, 8 years later, the Dow has more than tripled. Did those sellers ever get back in? Did they sell for short-term reasons when they should have been buying for long-term opportunity?

A SLICE OF LIFE—WITH PEPPERONI

Thomas Monaghan and his brother had a long-term vision in 1960. They believed if they could provide guaranteed fast, free delivery of hot pizza, they would beat any competition. They proceeded to figure out what it took to make pizza delivery work as a profitable business, which nobody else had at the time. Mr. Monaghan's brother, James, apparently developed a case of short-term thinking sometime before the long-term vision was realized. He swapped his share for a Volkswagen Beetle. Meanwhile, Thomas Monaghan stayed on for the long haul. He recently sold his company—Domino's Pizza—for an estimated $1 billion (that's billion, with a B)!

From the Winter 2001 Newsletter:

LOVE AND THE HAPPY DAYS

On February 25, 1972, an episode of Love, American Style entitled "Love and the Happy Days" aired on ABC television. Garry Marshall had produced a 1971 pilot called "New Family in Town" for ABC, and after they decided not to turn the pilot into a series, they decided to use it as a Love, American Style episode. After the success of George Lucas' film American Graffiti, the ABC programmers were looking to cash in on the wave of 1950s nostalgia. Remembering Garry Marshall's earlier pilot, they called him to make some changes to his original concept. Among the changes was to include the character of Arthur Fonzarelli. The rest of the Happy Days story is history.

Also in 1972, the Dow Jones Industrial Average was on its way to topping 1,000 for the first time in history, powered by the "nifty fifty"—stocks that could be bought at any price and held forever. Many believed that momentum would carry these stocks to perpetual new highs and that investing was easy. Sound familiar?

Alas, the next two years saw the Dow drop by over one-third, and for the five years from 1973 to 1977 the average annual compound return was a dismal 0.53 percent. The average annual returns for the S&P 500 and NASDAQ over that same five years were negative.

During that period of time, however, many investors made good money in well-managed mutual funds and carefully selected portfolios. Making money then involved extensive research and due diligence, along with disciplined and creative investment strategies. Investing today requires the same effort. It was not easy then, and it is not easy now.

Don't Give Up

In the midst of those economic dark days of the mid-1970s, great companies and industries were spawned, providing investors with plenty of profit potential. In 1974, Steven Jobs teamed up with Steve Wozniak to develop the first personal computer—the Apple I. In 1975, Bill Gates teamed up with Paul Allen to develop software for personal computers, and Microsoft was born. The rest is not only history, but continues to shape how we work and live.

From the current difficult economic and investment environment will emerge many great companies and industries that will also change the way we work and live. The risks to investors, like in the mid-1970s, are real, but the potential rewards are significant for those who not only have a well thought out plan, but stick to it.

From the Fall 2001 newsletter following the 9/11 terrorist attacks:

Different—Again

The stunning bull market of the 1990s swept most stocks higher. Some were propelled to stratospheric heights. Valuations surpassed even the wildest optimist's grandest expectations. During this period, investors allowed a lot of bad habits to creep into their approach to investing. The most dangerous was the notion that all the rules that guided investors for decades no longer applied. It was a new era for investing, with new rules. It was different. Then reality hit.

Sir John Templeton is supposed to have said that the four most dangerous words in investing are "this time is different." Nothing directly comparable to September 11 and its aftermath have ever happened in America, and so it would be all too easy for us to surrender again to this four-word synthesis.

Harry Truman said that the only thing new in the world is the history you don't know. But at a moment like this, when all seems different in terrible and threatening ways, we may conclude that the real danger to us is in the history we choose to ignore.

All real crises are new and different in some respects. Pearl Harbor surely appeared at the time to be something utterly without precedent in the American experience. So did the Cuban Missile Crisis, Vietnam, the Cambodian incursion, the killings at Kent State, the confluence of OPEC and Watergate, stagflation, the October 1987 stock market crash, and the Asian Contagion.

The one truly unprecedented thing in human history could be the success of the United States—its institution, its society, its economy, and its markets. This success is not separable from the crises we have encountered; it is, rather, a fabric woven out of those challenges, and out of our particular genius for mastering them.

REPEAT HISTORY

If history is any guide, you don't protect long-term investment capital by abandoning your investment plan, but by sticking to it. You thereby keep it exposed to the healing power of time—to the resilience of the American economy, and of the markets that reflect it.

Investment decisions based on long-term and even multigenerational financial goals usually turn out to be right, while current events–driven speculation on "what the market might do next" is usually wrong, and many people's lifetime plans never recover from it.

First, inflation is low and going lower, thanks to decreasing energy prices and improved efficiencies in production. Next, interest rates continue to decline, as the Fed recently dropped rates to their lowest level in thirty years and stands ready to take them lower still. Then, we have inventories. The well-publicized inventory glut has slowly been worked off, and we are near the point when firms will soon have to increase production to meet demand. Finally, income taxes have been reduced. A decline in all these factors is bullish for our economy—a situation that did not exist in previous slowdowns. While the economy may still have some rough sledding ahead, the ayes have it for an eventual recovery.

One of the positive results of recent events has been the renewed emphasis on that which is truly important and valuable. We cherish our freedom more. We appreciate our families and friends and neighbors more and hug our children a little more often. We are reevaluating our priorities and adjusting our lifestyles to reflect what is most important.

From the Summer 2013 Newsletter:

Lost in the Woods

The Philadelphia Flyers recently decided to part ways with goalie Ilya Bryzgalov. His erratic play was only surpassed by his erratic personality. Consider this quote about the universe: "I'm very into the universe, you know, like how was created, you know, like, what is it, you know? Solar system is so humongous big, right? But if you see like our solar system and our galaxy on the side, you know, like, we're so small you can never see it. Our galaxy is like huge, but if you see the big picture our galaxy [is] like a small tiny-like dot in the universe." In October 2011, following a wild 9-8 loss in Winnipeg, "Bryz" told reporters, "I'm lost in the woods right now" (USA Today, Oct. 28, 2011).

If you like volatility, the last couple of months were for you. Intraday moves of 100 or more points in the Dow Jones Industrial Average were common, as the market grasped the potential for the Federal Reserve to alter its credit policy. How much, when, and in what manner the Fed might change policy were the major issues in May and June. Traditionally "safe" or low-volatility investment options have been the most volatile, and we may have to come to grips with the potential for the markets to continue to slip lower in the weeks and months ahead.

Sticking with your plan and following your process should keep you from making emotional mistakes that could harm your long-term financial goals. If you really want to outperform the herd, you need to embrace corrections like this one. They set up buying opportunities. They allow different stocks and sectors to emerge as new market leaders. Keep your focus on the big picture—the universe—rather than the headlines, and you will not get lost in the woods.

What Did You Expect?

According to Flyers GM Paul Holmgren, Bryz played well for the Flyers and is still considered one of the better goalies available. So why would the team want to get rid of him? Because they expected much more since they were paying him a huge amount of money. With expectations so high, they were easily disappointed. Ryan Howard is paid a lot and expected to hit home runs for the Phillies. So even when he has a multi-hit game and knocks in runs, but does not hit a home run, fans are disappointed.

Expectations play a big part in investors' ability to stay with the disciplines necessary to implement the process to achieve their financial goals and objectives. Following the financial crises of 2008–09, many were happy to simply not lose money. In fact, most people did not even realize that the markets were recovering until recently. An annual survey of investors by Franklin Templeton Investments produced these results over the past several years. (thefool.com, May 22, 2013.)

- In 2010, 66 percent of investors said the S&P fell in 2009. Yet it was up 26 percent.
- In 2011, about half of investors said the market fell in 2010. Yet it was up 15 percent.
- In 2012, 53 percent of investors said the market fell in 2011. Yet it was up 2 percent.
- Recently, 31 percent of investors said the market fell last year. Yet it was up 16 percent.

No one can be blamed for having low expectations and believing that the stock market should be going down. In 2009, the economy was losing 700,000 jobs a month, GM and the major banks had to be bailed out, and the government ran a $1.4 trillion deficit. In 2011, Greece nearly collapsed; Congress nearly defaulted on the government's debt, which lost its AAA credit rating. According to Google, the phrase "double-dip recession" was mentioned in the media more than 10,000 times. At the end of last year, everyone was talking about the fiscal cliff and sequester. How could the market go up? Now that the markets have returned to their previous levels, expectations have been raised, and it is tempting to believe that the markets can only go up in the future. It is important to keep expectations realistic to avoid disappointment.

I will sum up this section by quoting William Arthur Ward, author of *Fountains of Faith* and one of America's most quoted writers of inspirational maxims. He said, "The pessimist complains about the wind; the optimist expects it to change; the realist adjusts the sails." Moving forward is difficult if you are continuously looking over your shoulder. An airplane is supposedly off course about 90 percent of the time, but the pilot does not turn around and start over, nor does he or she keep looking back. They make it to their final destination by nearly incessant course corrections throughout the duration of the flight.

You're going to get off track, either through your own doing or by unpredictable outside events. We may not be able to choose our circumstances, but we have 100 percent control over our reaction to them. You can choose to keep fighting the last war, or you can move forward with your plan. That choice belongs to you. Like the outlaw Josey Wales said at the end of the great movie starring Clint Eastwood about the Civil War, "I guess we all died a little in the damn war." And then he moved on.

MISTAKE # 3: BELIEVING THE CURRENT HYPE

We are surrounded and bombarded by experts and pundits touting the latest and greatest investment opportunities. Much of the "news" is really opinion dressed up to look like news. Much of the analysis is really entertainment dressed up to look like objective advice. Many of the "experts" on the business news programs are indeed very smart and well-meaning; however, they do not know you and your family and do not understand what you are trying to accomplish. They do not know how you got here, nor do they know where you want to go next. All I can say is: be careful out there!

Many "experts" tout model portfolios or show their investment program on their websites. They may seem like you, but their situations, goals, and objectives may be completely different. What if their income is higher than yours, so they could afford to take more risk? Or what if they had started earlier and been very fortunate to have accumulated more than they needed, so that they did not need to seek returns as high as you do to meet their goals? What if they could handle more risk and volatility? What would their plan mean to you? A doctor does not prescribe what he or she needs, but what they believe *you* need to stay healthy. A good financial advisor should do the same thing!

From Fall 2010 newsletter:

BUFFALO JUMP

A buffalo jump is a cliff formation which North American Indians historically used in mass killings of plains bison. The Native Americans used the bison for food, clothing, and shelter. Every part of the animal could be used in some way: hides for clothes and shelter, bones for tools, sinews for bowstrings and laces. Hooves could be ground for glue, and the brains could be used in the tanning process for hides. The trick was to get the bison to jump over the cliffs, breaking their legs and rendering them immobile so that the tribe members could close in with spears and bows. To do this, the most fleet-footed of the tribes would be disguised in robes of buffalo skin, show themselves to the buffalo, and run toward the cliff. Once near the edge, the young men would duck into a cranny while the bison all followed each other over the cliff. This may have been the first example of "following the herd."

From the Fall 1999 newsletter:

RUNNING OF THE BULLS

The original Bull, the new Bull, the bull market, the bull on CNBC. The original Bull is my brother Mark, who entered the world at 9 lbs., 11 oz. (mostly feet), and grew up to hit baseballs a great distance. The new Bull is my grandson Carson who, at seven and a half months, has thighs like tree trunks, multiple chins, and cheeks fat enough to suffocate him. The bull on CNBC has, unfortunately, distorted the public view of the bull market. The news reports would have us believe that the markets are at nosebleed heights—a speculative balloon ready to burst—and that millions of people have been simply raking in millions of dollars, especially day traders. All of the faithful CNBC watchers should keep in mind that it's only show business.

LIKE A LEAD BALLOON

The truth is that unless you've owned the largest capitalization stocks in the S&P or a handful of NASDAQ leaders, it hasn't been an easy stock market for most investors. If you removed the top ten stocks from the S&P 500 Index in 1998, the return would have been cut in half. If you took out the top five stocks in the NASDAQ, that index would have lost money in 1998. For the second year in a row, the average New York Stock Exchange stock is down. According to Ned Davis Research, only 20 percent of stocks have returned to their highs of April 1998, while the average stock is still down 20 percent since that time.

This difficult environment, combined with the revved-up expectations caused by the financial media, has frustrated a lot of investors. This includes day traders, 75 to 95 percent of whom lose money, according to one estimate.

From the Winter 2006 newsletter:

THE YEAR AHEAD

When I got into the office last Monday and could not find my notes, I remembered that I had brought my work home over the weekend to finish this newsletter. It was still in my briefcase, where I had placed it with good intentions on Friday evening. So I thought about the weekend and what I could write about that would be relevant.

On Saturday I noticed how crowded the gym was, and church was just as crowded on Sunday. The New Year must have everyone thinking about getting back in shape—physically and spiritually. While it was good to see everybody in both places, it made me think how important it is to pay attention to both body and soul every day throughout the year. The best way to do that is to plan ahead and implement that plan one step at a time, without regard to outside distractions or feelings. That is accomplished with investments through a financial plan and/or an investment policy statement, using strategic and tactical asset allocation. I will elaborate later.

Also over the weekend I read a wonderful article about Philadelphia native Jim Cramer, who can daily be found talking about money on CNBC. He is very entertaining, and his success story is very inspiring. I fear that many people, however, confuse entertainment with serious investment advice and follow him like a guru who will make them rich. That fear was reinforced when I got involved in a spirited game of Monopoly with my family on Sunday night. We played the dot-com version. If you are not familiar with that version, the streets of Atlantic City are replaced by dot-com companies. For example, instead of buying Boardwalk, you buy Yahoo!.

The most interesting part of the game to me is that the prices for everything are in millions and hundreds of millions, reflecting the outrageous valuations placed on companies during the dot-com mania. During that mania, there were gurus on TV providing entertainment that was confused with serious investment advice. The result for many was not good. I do not know this for a fact, but I suspect that the properties on the original Monopoly board are now worth more than the companies on the dot-com version. So be careful not to confuse entertainment with serious financial management and hot tips with a well-thought-out investment program. (By the way, I mean no disrespect to Mr. Cramer, and it is possible that a little "Mad Money," as his program is called, might have a place in a portfolio.)

From the Special Edition 1998 newsletter:

PESSIMISM—THE PREDICTABLE RESPONSE

When everything that is familiar to us starts to change or disappear, we become fearful and anxious about the future. That is precisely why most people, including the experts, have been so pessimistic over the past decades. Since the Berlin Wall came down and the "Evil Empire" was defeated (without firing a shot), capitalism has been spreading. But the New World Order is just that—new. And at times, that can be scary.

As late as World War I, virtually everything we now take for granted was unimaginable! Then, new technologies, industries, products, and services seemed to burst forth suddenly. Overnight, cars, phones, radios, electrical appliances, movies, Coca-Cola, and so much more became affordable, mainstream consumer items. Lindbergh made the first flight across the Atlantic. At the same time, that generation of consumers moved into their peak years of earning, spending, and productivity. That generation, like the baby boomers today, was augmented by a massive immigration wave that accelerated the boom. The Roaring 20s saw high economic growth, unprecedented 5 percent average gains in business productivity, a zero rate of inflation, rising savings rates, and falling debt ratios.

During and after World War I, we were pessimistic, and then along came the Roaring 20s. We were pessimistic during the Depression and World War II, and then along came the booming economy of the 1950s and 1960s. In the last two decades, beginning in the early 1970s, we have seen the advances in our standard of living slow down. During the 1991 recession, pessimism was once again rampant. Best-selling books predicting a dire future competed with one another on the list of New York Times bestsellers. The economy, and particularly the stock market, has been booming ever since.

From the Winter 1999 newsletter:

Haywire.com

Happy New Year. Following a year of violent swings, 1999 started out with a bang, followed by more volatility. I have not forgotten the daily sinking feeling in the pit of my stomach from August through October as all stocks looked to be headed for zero and most market commentators were constantly reinforcing that feeling.

In my Special Edition I urged calm, suggesting that the markets would recover and that the baby boom spending wave would continue to drive our economy. In relaying the theories of economist Henry Dent, Jr., I reported, "The Internet may be to the current era what the assembly line was to the Roaring 20s. It may be the key productivity lever that will rapidly feed new technologies, products, and services into the mainstream economy." I still believe that, but the current mania for anything Internet-related is unnerving. Be careful, and stay focused on your long-term goals and objectives.

To the Moon, Alice

Internet fever has sent the stocks of many companies toward the moon. This technological advancement may indeed someday be compared to innovations such as the steam engine and electricity. Yet, the total market capitalization of all Internet stocks is currently less than 2 percent of the economy, suggesting that as a group, they may have a long way to go. However, one needs to put the value of these companies in perspective. Online bookseller Amazon.com—which has yet to make a profit and is expected to lose more money next year—has a market capitalization of over $12 billion. That's five times the market cap of on-land book retailer Barnes & Noble, which has several times the revenue of its online rival and earned about $65 million last year. Yahoo!, which runs an Internet "portal" (a giant cyber-mall and media center) has a market cap of over $25 billion. Yahoo! has just turned profitable. Meanwhile, the New York Times Company, parent of what is arguably the world's most highly regarded general interest newspaper, with interests in broadcasting and information services and about three times the profit per share of Yahoo!, is valued at a paltry $6.6 billion. Shares of eBay, which had revenue of $12.9 million in the company's third quarter report, its first since going public, have a market value exceeding Federated Department Stores, which had third quarter revenue of $3.6 billion.

The urgency to invest in anything Internet may be premature. The "Net" is not a now-or-never proposition. Consider that while the first personal computer was shipped in 1978, Microsoft did not come onto the scene until 1986, and people who bought stock many years later still did just fine. There will be plenty of opportunities to invest in companies that will benefit from Internet usage at reasonable prices.

From the Fall 2002 newsletter:

BEAUTIFUL CHOICE

About four years ago, my daughter made a serious mistake by getting caught up with her emotions. The consequences would last a lifetime. Rather than compound her error, she sought the counsel and assistance of her parents and made some lifestyle adjustments. Although she was not instantly perfect, she did make a beautiful choice—life. The life she brought into the world, Carson, has almost single-handedly wrecked my house. He has kept me up at night, cost me plenty of money, and he knows he can get anything he wants from Pop-Pop. The joy that he has brought into my life is priceless.

RENEWED DISCIPLINE

About three years ago, many investors made serious mistakes by getting caught up with their emotions. The consequences have been dire. Old-fashioned, time-tested principals like diversification, asset allocation, and prudent research were labeled outdated. CEOs of companies with no earnings were being idolized and celebrated, while "value" investors were being laughed at. Every investor has now suffered from the fallout. But those investors who seek professional guidance and counsel, who make prudent adjustments to their portfolios and make choices based on sound investment discipline during these difficult times, will ultimately have a much better chance of meeting their objectives.

From the Winter 2013 newsletter, when the hype was that the world would end on December 21, 2012:

STILL STANDING

The fact that you are reading this means that the world did not end on 12/21/12. However, that does not mean that the world as we once knew it did not end. At least, it changed so much as to challenge the way we interpret and react to events as investors. Is there, in fact, a new normal, or are we just waiting to "revert to the mean"? PIMCO's bond king, Bill Gross, recently proclaimed the "cult of equity is dying." Gross wrote in his August Investment Outlook that stock investors should think again about the age-old buy-and-hold investing mantra. He says consistent, annual returns are a thing of the past. In his view, investors' impressions of "stocks for the long run" or any run have mellowed. (wsj.com/marketpulse, July 31, 2012).

You might not remember the "cult of equity" as well as I do, since being in my business makes me more sensitive to it. Following a run through the 1980s and into the 1990s, with a pause in the middle, equities, as measured by the

DJIA, had risen from a low of less than 1,000 to over 14,000. This culminated in the tech bubble in the year 2000—when Y2K was supposed to end the world as we knew it then. In the five years ending in early 2000, the NASDAQ, which contained many of these technology stocks, had increased over five times. Everyone seemed to be talking about the stock market and which technology stocks would be the next "hot dot." Every TV at the gym or club was set on CNBC, which became a phenomenon during this time. Risk management, diversification, asset allocation, and long-term planning were only for those who did not understand how to make money in the "new economy." What followed was the lost decade, which culminated with the financial meltdown in 2008. Individuals have been withdrawing money from equity funds in record amounts ever since.

History Lesson

The last time the death of equities was announced was in a 1979 cover article in Business Week magazine (August 13, 1979). That article stated that millions of shareholders had defected from the stock market over the decade of the 1970s, leaving equities more than ever the province of giant institutional investors. The implications for the US economy, therefore, could not be worse, with even the institutions still in the financial markets pouring money into short-term investments and alternate equity investments. This death of equity was something, according to the article, that no stock market rally would correct.

Younger investors, in particular, were avoiding stocks. Between 1970 and 1975, the number of investors declined in every age group but one: individuals sixty-five and older. While the number of investors under sixty-five dropped by about 25 percent, the number of investors over sixty-five jumped by more than 30 percent. **"Only the elderly, who have not understood the changes in the nation's financial markets or who are unable to adjust to them, are sticking with stocks."** The emphasis is mine.

So in 1979, close to the bottom in equity prices, the only people who stuck with stocks were those who did not understand what was going on. In 2000, at the height of the tech bubble and beginning of the lost decade, only those who did not understand were getting out of growth stocks.

HISTORY REPEATS

So where are we today? According to a recent article, people are withdrawing money from equities in record numbers again and have lost faith in stocks. (AP IMPACT: "Ordinary Folks Losing Faith in Stocks," December 27, 2012.)

I am not making any predictions, but this all sounds familiar.

A good summary from the Fall 1999 newsletter:

BALANCE, FOCUS, POWER

In The Karate Kid, Mr. Miyagi explained to his student, Daniel, the key to karate and to life: balance, focus, power. In karate, a balanced stance and focus on the target results in a powerful punch. In life, a balance between work and play, with focus on one's goals, results in a powerful existence. With investing, the same principles apply. A balanced portfolio with a focus on one's long-term goals will bring, over time, powerful results. Many market commentators, instead of encouraging people to focus on their long-term goals and objectives with a well-thought-out plan and balanced portfolio, are drawing their focus to short-term results and daily events.

MISTAKE #4: NOT PAYING FOR PROTECTION

I was the quarterback for my high school football team. We ran an offense that threw the ball a lot, and I enjoyed some success. However, I could not have completed any passes without the protection of my teammates on the offensive line. You cannot live in your house without paying for the protection from calamity that your homeowner's insurance policy provides. If you have an auto accident, even if you are not at fault, your auto insurance company is there to make you whole and get you back on the road. It is just as important to have someone there to protect you and to help get you get back on the road to meeting your financial goals in the event of a financial calamity. The price you pay for these protections is small compared to the potential cost of not having them. I believe it is imperative for someone to have your back when it comes to the financial future of you and your family.

From the Summer 1999 newsletter:

> ### No Respect
>
> Recent ads for online brokerages suggest that bartenders can make multi-million-dollar bids for companies, tow truck drivers can buy their own islands, and teenagers can afford helicopters simply by trading online. They also imply—actually they state bluntly—that full-service brokers are boorish, selfish morons who give only bad advice and do not care about the customer. While some of my brethren may fit that description, there may also be some doctors, lawyers, and CPAs who fall into the same category.
>
> My sense of humor is keen, and I have chuckled at some of these ads, but I am beginning to think that some people actually believe them! I have written previously about the

wonders of the Internet. Online trading is one of them, as it allows individuals who are comfortable making their own investment decisions to invest economically and easily. Of course, there are some people who can do this, but according to recent studies, most people are not effective at investing on their own. There is far too much financial information for the average investor to sort through in order to make tough financial decisions.

The Modern Way

Technology has transformed the way we do business and interact with customers. The Internet and intranets are ushering in a "network revolution" where organizations and industries are being run from the customer back, not the top down. It's not just about streamlining an organization to make it a little more responsive. In the network economy, customers drive the system, not producers.

Most serious investors want one objective human "browser" to understand their unique goals and risk tolerances and to customize a portfolio and investment system to insure that they meet their financial goals. That means coordinating expertise in insurance, taxes, and a broad array of investment options. It means representing the investor, not the investments to be sold, to provide objective advice.

From the Fall 1999 newsletter:

Everybody Wants Some

Everybody wants and should receive financial advice. But everybody should not receive the same financial advice. One person's investment information can be another person's misinformation. Information alone, delivered indiscriminately, is not enough.

Your financial needs are as individual as your signature. Rather than trying to fit you into a prepackaged portfolio of accounts and services, my mission is to provide flexible, innovative, and imaginative solutions expertly suited to meet your short- and long-range goals. You deserve customized products and services handled with confidentiality and convenience.

From the Winter 2000 newsletter:

Opportunity Knocked

The cost of missing out on an opportunity is appropriately known as the opportunity cost. While I was cleaning out the guns, canned goods, and bottled water from my Y2K bunker, I pondered the opportunities that were missed by those who were snookered by the media hype into worrying about a problem that billions of dollars had already gone toward fixing. It is the same media that obsesses over the costs associated with investing and causes many investors, or potential investors, to miss out on wonderful opportunities because they are focused on fees, commissions, and surrender charges. These costs are a small price to pay for receiving personal, caring service from a trained, experienced advisor supported by research and information from multiple sources. So while the media pounds away at the expenses associated with enjoying objective, customized services from an advisor, keep in mind that the largest cost is often missing the benefits that person can provide.

From the Winter 2001 newsletter:

FOOLISH ADVICE

There are some foolish guys out there—Motley Fools—who have made a living bashing people like me. They wear funny hats and claim that you should never pay for the services of a financial professional when you can follow their advice, which has, in the fools' words, "obliterated the playing field as the Rule Breaker Portfolio has done." They established their reputation by picking some technology stocks early—not by helping real people with real-life situations. They dismissed the advice of professionals as "hogwash" while touting their performance and promoting their stocks during the tech bull rally. However, this past year, their highly touted Rule Breaker Portfolio lost over 50 percent. Their response was that they did not mean for anyone to actually follow their advice or really buy their stocks, but only to follow along for educational purposes. (They recently reevaluated their mission.) I know this should not bother me, but in the words of Rocky Balboa when asked if Apollo Creed's mocking on TV bothered him, "It did."

A FOOL FOR YOU

Your situation is real. I cannot change the rules, reevaluate my mission, or rework my track record after a bad year. I cannot claim to have only been educating you, not really expecting you to do what I recommended. I have too much respect and compassion for you to do that. Besides, it would be foolish.

From the Fall 2011 newsletter:

Foolish Advice

A lot of people lost a lot of money because they got caught up in investing as a form of recreation. Several years ago, a couple of fools started an online investment service. They convinced a lot of people that investing was easy, fun, and profitable (as long as you followed their advice). They warned against seeking financial advice from someone with something to sell while plastering their website with ads for fund groups and brokers they recommended.

Now they claim that something has been missing—someone to provide personal, customized financial advice. They now recognize that most people are busy with their careers and family and do not have the time or training necessary to come up with solutions to their financial needs. They are announcing this revelation to introduce a new service and charge an additional fee, but you already recognized the value of a full-service financial professional.

From the Winter 2002 newsletter:

Give Peace a Chance

John Lennon once lamented that "Everybody's talking ..." and all he was saying was "give peace a chance." The Super Bowl was really a great game, but the game itself was lost in all the chatter and banter before and after (including the halftime duet with Terry Bradshaw and Paul McCartney singing "A Hard Day's Night"). There was more talk the next day about which commercials were the funniest or most creative than there was about the game itself. Before

President Bush even delivered the State of the Union address, reporters spent the whole day dissecting and analyzing what they thought he might say.

Every morning you can watch and listen as one analyst after another tells what may happen, could happen, or should happen on Wall Street, and what you may, could, or should do about it—before the market even opens. You can find out all about having the courage to be rich, or the nine steps to financial freedom from an "expert" selling her wares through infomercials. Or you could seek peace of mind by relying upon an established relationship with someone who understands your needs.

I HAVE YOUR BACK—ALWAYS

When my middle daughter, Cerissa, was in high school, she had a disagreement with a friend of hers over a boy (what else?). The argument evidently escalated to the point where she became the victim of bullying, before the term "bullying" was in vogue, by some of the other girl's friends. One Saturday night as I got under the covers to fall asleep watching *Saturday Night Live*, the doorbell rang, and it was my daughter's friend wanting to talk to my daughter. I went downstairs, reasoned with her, and walked her out to her car. I didn't notice at first that there were two other cars out there until about five boys walked out from behind the bushes planning to ambush my daughter but surrounding me instead.

There I was, in my slippers and bathrobe with my skinny legs sticking out and my hair all messed up, surrounded by a group of teenagers looking for a fight. I only could think of one thing to do. I said, "Okay, let's go, one at a time—who wants to go first?" Thinking I must be crazy, they got into their cars and took off.

Cerissa's friend came back later with her father to apologize, and they have been good friends ever since.

After my son, Jon Jr., graduated from college, he played in a summer baseball league, and I helped coach (of course). One night the game got a little out of hand. We had a big lead, and tempers began to get frayed between the players and the fans. The other team had some fans who had evidently been consuming adult beverages. I was coaching first base, and my friend was coaching third base right in front of the other team's dugout. In the midst of a lot of chirping between their players and our third base coach, one of our players hit a home run and proceeded to flip the bat and trot slowly around the bases, a show of disrespect for the other team.

Next up was my son, probably facing a bean ball. However, before the next pitch was thrown, one of the drunken fans ran onto the field and went after our third base coach. With that, my son ran to protect him, followed by the catcher, who went after my son. I made a beeline toward the catcher, a stud half my age, to protect my son. Both benches emptied, and when the dust settled I had him pinned up against the fence. We canceled the game at that point, and all of our players got a big kick out of crazy Coach Leise acting like a fool. As we all got into our cars to go home, my cell phone rang. It was my son, who said, "Thanks for having my back."

"Always, son, always," I replied.

Where do I get the urge to protect those I love? Where else but from my father? He was easy-going, but he had a line that he would not let people cross when it came to his loved ones. Once, when I was around ten years old, he told me to rake the back and side yard while he took his afternoon nap. He suggested I rake the neighbor's yard also because it was the right thing to do. I raked all of the leaves from both yards to the curb, some in front of our house and some in front of our neighbor's. I went back in the house feeling pretty good about myself until the doorbell rang. It was our neighbor, furious that I had left some leaves in front of his house and demanding that I correct the situation. As he was yelling at me, he entered our house. I turned around to see my normally easy-going father standing next to me in the living room in his underwear, hair all messed up, demanding to know what the problem was. When he was informed, he got right into the neighbor's face and ordered him out of the house. He told him in no uncertain terms that if he ever threatened me again, there would be hell to pay. The neighbor left. As my father went back upstairs, I knew he would always have my back.

Years later, I was taking the train to college after my first trip home for Thanksgiving. I would get on at the 30th Street station in Philadelphia and take the train back to Lancaster, Pennsylvania. My parents drove me to the train and walked me to the platform to see me off. The station was crowded, and we headed up the escalator to the platform, which was even more crowded. My dad and I got to the platform first and turned around to see my mother unable to get off of the escalator because of the crowd. She had a look of fear in her eyes as she called my father's name. With that, he turned around and shoved the whole crowd of people about six feet.

I got on the train knowing again that my father would have our backs, especially my mother's. I knew that firsthand because once I had sassed my mother and jumped out of the car, heading into my then-girlfriend's house. As I walked up the sidewalk I felt something bumping me. It was my father, who had driven the car up on the sidewalk and was driving into me. He leaned his head out of the window and told me, "You don't sass your mother, so apologize." I knew he was serious. I apologized, and it never happened again!

Why am I telling theses stories? Because I consider my clients like my family and will go to great lengths to have their backs. Why is it important that you have a financial advisor who has your back, rather than a planner who gives you a plan and sends you on your way? Consider these examples.

From the Summer 2001 newsletter:

> ### Step #7 of Seven Steps to Investing with Less Risk: Seek Professional Guidance.
>
> "The bridge to success is never crossed alone." Most serious investors are looking for advice from someone who can find unique solutions to their unique needs and objectives. I am committed to staying armed with as much education, knowledge, and technology as possible so as to provide a highly personal, caring, and attentive relationship; a wide array of research and information from multiple sources; a superior choice of fairly priced, high-quality investment options; flexible cost structures, including fee-based alternatives to deliver the best value; and objective and customized services.

From the Winter 1998 newsletter:

> ### Emotional Rescue
>
> The meltdown in Asia and subsequent 500-point drop in the Dow, while a white-knuckle experience, provided an opportunity for me to lend some rational, objective advice and emotional support. To those of you who called me early in the morning, late at night, during the day, at home, in the car, and in the office—thank you! It felt good to be needed! My best compliment came from a client who said he could sleep soundly during market turbulence because

he knew I was awake worrying. (He also still has all of his hair, while I don't!)

From the Spring 2010 newsletter:

"WE JUST WASTED TWO MILLION BUCKS"

During the peak of tech stock mania in 2000, within months of that bubble bursting, one online brokerage firm ran an ad during the Super Bowl which featured a chimpanzee lip-synching the song "La Cucaracha" with the tagline, "Well, we just wasted two million bucks. What are you doing with your money?"

At the time, the firm was involved in several legal disputes with clients who alleged that their ads inflated expectations for investment returns. The previous year, the SEC chairman had publicly criticized online brokers' ads for potentially appearing to promise riches. This year, the same firm is featuring talking babies and ridiculing full-service advisors. The ads are pretty funny, but when it comes to helping investors meet their long-term goals and objectives, I am dead serious.

While the financial markets have recovered quite a bit over the past year, there are still many investors who are behind in their retirement and investment plans. There is still a lot of serious work to do. While the talking babies are having fun ridiculing advisors, Fidelity Investments' Third Annual Millionaire Outlook found that millionaires credit their advisors with helping limit losses and cope with the financial crisis. According to the study's findings, "millionaires have clearly benefited from the expertise, calming influence, and reassuring role advisors often play, particularly during periods of uncertainty" (Fidelity Investments, June 29, 2009). I do not know for a fact, but I suspect that no one from the firms running the ads, or their ad agencies, has ever lost any sleep worrying about your financial future. I do know for a fact that I have.

My Promise to You

Your advisor, whether you are a millionaire or not, promises to take the following steps going forward to help you get where you want to be and stay there:

- Stay armed with as much education, knowledge, and technology as possible.
- Be proactive in identifying opportunities as the markets present them, consistent with your specific goals and objectives.
- Continue to prudently expand my team to provide a deeper lineup with more diverse life experience and educational backgrounds.
- Exercise and maintain a proper diet so I can stay alert and healthy to put in the time and effort necessary.
- Stay excited about the business I am in and take advantage of every opportunity to improve.
- Give back to causes that are important to my family, my friends, and my clients.

I have found that if I can help a person avoid just one stupid mistake, I can have an immeasurable affect on their financial life.

From the Winter 2007 newsletter:

What, Me Worry?

Could anything go wrong when most indicators seem positive? Of course! But why worry about it? That is what you pay me to do. Worry doesn't rid tomorrow of its sorrows; it only robs today of its joys. Plus, when you make a mountain out of a molehill, you may end up having to climb it.

This reminds me of the salesman who usually drove an old car and wore outdated clothing. One day he showed up for work in a Mercedes-Benz and wearing a tailored suit. "What happened?" his co-workers asked. He replied, "I hired a team of professional worriers. Now I tell them my problems, and they do all the worrying while I go out and sell." His friends wanted to know how much they charged. "$5,000 a week." When they asked how he could afford that much, he replied, "That's their worry, not mine!"

I worry about what could go wrong so that you do not have to. You can spend your time making a living, advancing your career, enjoying your family, doing volunteer work, traveling, golfing, reading, watching TV, or whatever it is that you would rather do than read the financial pages. It is my pleasure and the business I have chosen. My challenge is to stay armed with as much education, information, and resources as possible to make sure you can meet your financial needs and objectives.

OTHER MISTAKES TO AVOID

From the Summer 2007 newsletter:

Little Mistakes

One recent evening I took in two baseball games (what a surprise). First I watched my grandson Carson play a coach-pitch all-star game. That game was highlighted by two arguments between the umpire and coaches and three ejections. One of the players inadvertently threw his bat following a swing, and the ump felt compelled to toss him out of the game. This turned out to be a mistake, as two more kids threw their bats and had to be ejected to follow precedent. The coaches argued that this was all unnecessary since the kids are only eight years old. The umpire's mistake had ruined an otherwise enjoyable evening.

I left that excitement for my older son Jonathon's game. His summer league is pretty laid back, so there were no arguments or ejections. He was brought in to pitch the last two innings. He had not pitched since Little League but was up for the challenge. He proceeded to put down the first five batters in order and had two strikes on the last batter ready to end the game. I was thoroughly enjoying myself and looking for him to throw a "waste" pitch when, instead, he threw a fastball right down the middle that the batter hit right over the centerfield fence. He got the next batter out, but that mistake spoiled an otherwise perfect outing.

Big Mistakes

Investors can ruin an otherwise well-thought-out financial plan by making one of the Eight Great Mistakes. (For a more detailed discussion of these mistakes, call me to receive a copy of *Simple Wealth, Inevitable Wealth* by Nick Murray.) These eight mistakes are the most common and can cause the most damage.

OVERDIVERSIFICATION: Owning nothing by owning everything. This happens when, rather than building a portfolio, one buys anything that sounds good. Over time, you have a collection of stuff instead of a well-thought-out, broadly diversified portfolio.

UNDERDIVERSIFICATION: The fatal narrowing of a portfolio down to essentially one idea. By trying to own only what is going up at any particular time, you may end up with only what is going down when the tide turns.

EUPHORIA: The loss of an adult sense of principal risk (also known as greed). This happens when we think that as a stock rises, its risk of a significant decline diminishes, causing people to buy high.

PANIC: The failure of faith in the face of the apocalypse of the day (also known as fear). This is the opposite of euphoria and causes us to sell low.

SPECULATING INSTEAD OF INVESTING: The siren song of a "new era." Buying into hype about a new product, new paradigm, cure for cancer, oil discovery, etc. A stock certificate is not a lottery ticket.

INVESTING FOR YIELD INSTEAD OF TOTAL RETURN: Financial suicide on the installment plan by fixing one's income in the face of many years of rising living costs. This happens when one tries to take 6 percent a year from an asset (like a CD or bond) that can only return 6 percent a year, rather than an asset like equities, which has historically returned

8 to 10 percent per year (past performance is no guarantee of future results).

LETTING YOUR COST BASIS DICTATE YOUR INVESTMENT DECISIONS: This can happen because of one great stock that you refuse to sell and pay capital gains taxes, or a lousy stock that you cannot stand to take a loss on. Your investments do not know what you paid for them.

LEVERAGE: Hawking the house to buy the wrong idea at the wrong time. Leverage makes sense in theory, but it is often used in tandem with previous mistakes, thus magnifying their disastrous effects.

CHAPTER FOUR

Making Work Optional

SPECIAL RISKS AROUND RETIREMENT

"Thirty-six percent of American workers age fifty-five to sixty-four say they have less than $25,000 in retirement savings." —Employee Benefit Research Institute (2014)

"Fifty-one percent of households are at risk of not having enough savings to maintain their standard of living after retirement." —The Center for Retirement Research at Boston College (2014)

"Sixty-six percent of Americans said their top financial concern was not having enough money for retirement." —Gallup poll (2014)

THE RISKIEST DAY OF YOUR LIFE

Many of the 79 million baby boomers retiring over the next few years will face unprecedented challenges in maintaining their standard of living in retirement. Middle-income Americans are most at risk, as longer life spans, the decline of guaranteed sources of retirement income, and the fact that nearly half of older Americans lack employer-based retirement plans contribute to increased retirement risk. Retirement in the United States traditionally rested on a three-legged stool consisting of pensions, Social Security, and personal savings.

The first leg was a pension provided by the individual's employer, which promised a fixed income for the rest of one's life based upon a predetermined formula. This was known as a defined benefit. The second leg of the stool was Social Security. This was also a promise, from the government, of income for life that was indexed to inflation and based upon a predetermined formula. Individuals could then supplement these sources of guaranteed lifetime income with interest on their personal savings, the third leg.

This three-legged stool has come under pressure over the past twenty-five years. At the same time, more companies began offering defined contribution plans—401(k)s, IRAs, and profit-sharing plans—where the future benefit was unknown, but the contribution was defined, normally as a percentage of income. In 1980, 28 percent of the workforce was covered by a defined benefit pension plan. Twenty years later, by 2000, less than 7 percent were covered. Furthermore, following the financial crisis in 2008, several large employers found themselves unable to keep the promises they made to employees. They severely reduced or even eliminated their pension payments to existing retirees. In addition, the economy and financial markets have experienced increasing uncertainty and volatility, putting personal savings at risk. Meanwhile, Social Security has come under attack as a bloated entitlement program that is growing more expensive and less financially viable, as people live longer and the ratio of current workers and contributors to the plan shrinks in relation to the number of recipients. This suggests that future retirees may be faced with reduced benefits from Social Security.

Your retirement date may actually be the riskiest day of your life. At that point, you are the most vulnerable to market declines because your wealth is likely at its peak. The five years before and after retirement are often referred to as the retirement red zone. Mistakes made during this time could cause disastrous and irreparable damage to your lifestyle. The results would not be mere setbacks; they would be life-altering mistakes that could result in having to scale back retirement dreams, sell a home, or go back to work.

From the Fall 2004 newsletter:

BACK TO SCHOOL

A lot of emotional events happened this month as the crowd subsided at the Leise residence. Jonathon began his career at Rider, Jael went back to Bloomsburg for her senior year, Jake moved up to high school, and Carson got on the bus for kindergarten. Debby and I tried our best to enjoy each milestone and stay composed. For me, though, the emotions hit their peak as Junior prepared to leave.

On the Saturday before his departure, we went over to Union Field for one more batting practice to get him ready. It was on that field where he had played and I had coached so many games. Over the past ten years, I estimate, conservatively, that I have thrown well over 500,000 pitches to Junior and his teammates. This would be the last time. Afterward, as we walked around the field picking up balls, I thought of all the key hits, home runs, and diving catches he made on that field. I remembered all of the times I suffered along with him when he made an out, and all of the championships I had shared with him and his special group of friends. They were all moving on, and my time with them as their coach and mentor was over.

I watched my little boy (all six feet, two inches of him) get into his car and drive away, and I wondered what kind of job I had done coaching and preparing him for the next level of baseball and the next phase of his life. Did I teach him everything he would need to be successful? Did I push him too hard or not hard enough? Will he be okay? I hope I did a good job, but there are no guarantees.

Life Goes On

As traumatic and final as Junior's last batting practice was, I was back at Union Field the very next day to run practice for Jake's team. So life goes on. This made me think of all of the people who work and save and invest all of their lives to prepare for retirement. When that day arrives, they are finished with one phase of life and can only wonder if they have prepared properly for the next level. And there are no guarantees.

The very next day they begin a new phase of life that may last as long as the previous one. If they have not prepared properly, that retirement phase may not be so pleasant, and they may even be forced to return to the previous phase (employment) and try it again.

SOMETIMES THERE IS NO TOMORROW

The accumulation phase of investing can be forgiving. As a matter of fact, if you simply stay invested in a diversified portfolio, keep adding to it systematically (dollar-cost-average), rebalance periodically, and avoid too many of the mistakes detailed in the previous chapters, you may do fine. Many mistakes can be made up for over time. However, there comes a point when time is running out, when mistakes can not only be costly, but can completely destroy what has been accomplished up until that point. In the words of Apollo Creed to a tiring, lazy Rocky Balboa in Rocky III: "THERE IS NO TOMORROW! THERE IS NO TOMORROW! THERE IS NO TOMORROW!"

From the Summer 2014 newsletter:

BETTER LIVING THROUGH TV

In 1922, over the objections of congressmen and cultural commentators, AT&T announced that its network of radio stations would be adding commercials to their broadcasts, effectively ending the era when radio was the province of hobbyists and amateur showmen. Twenty-eight years later, Hazel Bishop's $50,000-a-year cosmetics company proved the effectiveness of advertising when it placed ads in the few markets that had television and within two years saw business expand nearly 9,000 percent (avclub.com, Noel Murray, March 11, 2010).

In 1955, a Brooklyn bus driver named Ralph Kramden bought 2,000 all-in-one kitchen gadgets for $200 and booked time on TV to sell them. Ralph, though, was fictional. In Season 1, Episode 7 of The Honeymooners, "Better Living Through Television," Ralph's newest get-rich-quick scheme is to sell the all-purpose kitchen gadget with his buddy Ed Norton's assistance. Ralph plans to demonstrate it during live on TV, but his last-minute stage fright ruins the commercial. The episode contains some Honeymooners standbys. There are jokes about Ralph's weight. (When

Ralph warns Alice that he could always leave her and that "you can't place your arms around a memory," she stares at his belly and snaps, "I can't even put my arms around you.") There are jokes about Ralph's haplessness. (Both Norton and Alice quip that to find someone dumb enough to buy this gadget, all Ralph has to do is knock on his own door.) When the commercial is scheduled to air, Ralph, the "chef of the future," comes roaring into the mock kitchen looking like a bug-eyed maniac, ditches the prepared script, and just defaults to his interjections, "Ha-ha!" and "Ooooooh!" Ralph's quivering "chef of the future" tries to show off the modern way to "core a apple," and leaves the fruit in shambles.

Better Living through Planning

Ralph Kramden was always looking for an easy way to have a better life. Unfortunately, accumulating, preserving, and distributing wealth is not easy. It's a long-term endeavor that requires planning, discipline, and the assistance of a qualified, caring financial professional. The accumulation stage is simpler and more forgiving, yet requires the discipline to spend less than one earns and then put the difference in a position to grow and multiply.

The task becomes more difficult during the preservation, distribution, and legacy planning stage. This is when many people enter the "work is optional" chapter of their lives (commonly known as retirement). At this point, what many people fail to realize is that their investment portfolio has in essence become their employer. If they choose to take on this task alone, they are employing themselves to become the pension fund manager for themselves and their family's future.

In 2011 the Phillies had the best record in baseball going into the playoffs. They faced a Cardinals team that barely made it into the playoffs in a best-of-five series. The playoffs are like retirement. During a long season, there are many ups and downs, and a lot of mistakes are made along the way. Just like with investing, too many mistakes can accumulate to keep a team out of the playoffs, but many mistakes can be made up for over time. The Phillies made fewer mistakes than other teams that year and began the playoffs with a win over the underdog Cardinals.

In the second game, the Phillies took a 4–0 lead into the fourth inning and knocked Cardinals ace Chris Carpenter out of the game early. Things looked pretty good. Then, in the fourth inning, I watched in horror as Cliff Lee, who was 7–2 in the postseason and 3–0 in the League Division Series, coughed up the lead. The offense also went dead, and the Phillies lost 4–3. After splitting the next two games, the fifth and final game featured both team's aces—Roy Halliday for the Phillies and Chris Carpenter for the Cardinals. For the loser, there was no tomorrow.

Halladay made only one mistake—giving up a triple to the first batter, who scored the game's one and only run. The Phillies were stunned, and the Cardinals went on to win the World Series. That's not all. Since that game, the Phillies organization has been in a steady decline. I now watch the games along with only about half the number of fans that attended in 2011, and the team is in last place. (I still cheer for my team and refuse to boo.) A few mistakes when *there is no tomorrow* can ruin a great season and equally ruin a great investment plan!

From the Spring 2006 newsletter:

WHEN I'M SIXTY-FOUR

"When I get older, losing my hair, many years from now."
Paul McCartney wrote that when he was a teenager and

a Beatle. He looked far into the future and saw himself "doing the garden, digging the weeds" and "yours sincerely, wasting away." His questions, "Will you still need me? Will you still feed me?" will be answered this June when he will, in fact, turn sixty-four!

Now that he is hitting that milestone, he has found that sixty-four is not really so old after all. He is the father of a three-year-old, recently released a new album, and is reportedly going on tour later this year. Speaking of rockers in their sixties, when Mick Jagger of the Rolling Stones introduced "Satisfaction" during their performance at the Super Bowl, he correctly pointed out that they could have played that song at the first Super Bowl forty years ago. Jagger will turn sixty-three this July while he and the Stones will be performing in Europe. They are "still surviving on the streets" and touring all over.

Rather than retiring to a rocking chair like Whistler's mother, who was only forty-nine when her son painted her famous portrait, today's seasoned citizens are active and productive. Joe Paterno led Penn State to within one second of a perfect season and a successful Orange Bowl appearance at the age of seventy-eight. Jack McKean led the Florida Marlins to a World Series title at seventy-two. Barbara Walters hosts The View at seventy-six. Alan Greenspan chaired the Fed until age seventy-eight. Average life expectancy has increased by thirty years over the past century. That's the good news.

Seventy-seven million baby boomers will be reaching what used to be retirement age—sixty—in the coming years. They will be looking to continue their current standard of living or better for another thirty to forty years. Most of them will have 401(k) plans with between $500,000 and $1,000,000. That's where the bad news comes in. These folks face risks that the generation before them did not:

- Inflation risk—loss of purchasing power;
- Longevity risk—outliving their assets; and
- Investment risk—too aggressive, too conservative, or poor timing.

According to Ibbotson Associates, Inc., a portfolio of 50 percent Large Company Growth Stocks and 50 percent Intermediate Term Bonds invested at year-end 1972 with an initial 5 percent annual withdrawal rate adjusted for 3 percent inflation would have lasted for approximately twenty-two years. However, if inflation were 4 percent, that money would have run out in about twelve years. Also, many future seasoned citizens will be lacking something that the generation before them took for granted—guaranteed pensions.

THE HISTORY OF RETIREMENT

- 1601: English Poor Law is the first to hold that the state should provide for its citizens. Features taxation to support the destitute.
- 1818: Service Pension Law provides that every person who had served in the Revolutionary War would receive a fixed pension for life.
- 1875: The American Express Company implements the first private pension plan in the United States.
- 1880: Baltimore and Ohio Railroad establishes the first pension plan financed by both employer and employee contributions.

- 1882: Alfred Dodge Company withholds 1 percent of each worker's pay and puts it into a pension fund, to which Dodge adds 6 percent interest each year.
- 1935: The Social Security Act creates a program to pay workers age sixty-five and older a continuing income after retirement.
- 1974: IRAs are created.
- 1981: 401(k)s come into being.
- 2006: Verizon, IBM, and GM are among companies freezing pension plans.
- 2018: The first year in which the Social Security Board of Trustees projects tax revenues will fall below the program's costs.

In the rush to gain control over our financial lives through defined contribution plans—IRAs, 401(k)s, 403(b)s, etc.—few noticed that employers were in as much of a hurry to eliminate defined benefit plans, or pensions. This transfer of responsibility exposes us to the three risks stated above and increases our "probability of ruin."

From the Summer 2014 newsletter:

Planning to Make Work Optional

The idea of institutionalized retirement is an Industrial Age social experiment that may have run its course. The scheme of forcing the issue of retirement at a particular age was hatched by Chancellor Otto von Bismarck in the 1800s in Germany. At the time, retirement was mandated at the age of seventy, although the average German worker then did not live past age forty-six. Ironically, von Bismarck was seventy-four. The concept was imported to our country during the Depression as a lever to move older people out of the workforce to make way for younger workers. Del Webb later invented the term "golden-ager" with the goal of having lots of money and nothing to do but play. Over time, however, many people found that they could retire with means but very little meaning. A recent Rand study noted the "diminishing law of returns on leisure" as a chief capstone of an emerging "un-retirement" trend. Dying rich cannot compete with living rich, and making a living does not measure up to making a life (Financial Advisor Magazine, 2014).

Make My Day

At eighty-four, Clint Eastwood isn't sitting on his laurels, taking naps and complaining about his Social Security. He's still in the game and an inspiration for anybody worried about growing old. He offered the Associated Press this retirement planning advice: "You're not too old to do anything." Age has made him a better director, Eastwood says. "You have more experience as you get older. You can play on that if you're lucky enough genetically or you take good enough care of yourself."

The next time you're feeling like you're on the downward slide, let this wisdom attributed to Eastwood make your day: "I'd like to be a bigger and more knowledgeable person ten years from now than I am today. I think that, for all of us, as we grow older, we must discipline ourselves to continue expanding, broadening, learning, keeping our minds active and open" (Bankrate.com, 2014).

SERIOUS MISTAKES

That brings me to the most serious risks people face and most costly mistakes people make when in the retirement red zone. You cannot afford to ignore these risks! There is no tomorrow! There is no tomorrow!

From the Fall 2012 newsletter:

New Generation

Turning sixty-five was once linked only to retirement, early bird specials, gray Velcro shoes, and maybe moving to Del Boca Vista. The current generation is living and working longer, and through a combination of healthier diets, exercise, and Botox, resisting the aging process. Eventually, however, most will transition from active employment into some form of retirement, semi-retirement, or a second career that is more about fulfillment and less about money. When that transition occurs, there are four basic needs that still need to be met:

- Replacing your paycheck;
- Continuing to get raises;
- Protecting your family with health benefits; and
- Preparing to pass your assets to the next generation.

New Rules

Previous generations had very simple rules for retirement planning:

- Buy a house because it will be worth ten times more when you sell it.
- Buy and hold blue chip stocks—they will make you rich.
- When you retire, put your money in bonds or CDs and live off the interest.

- Work for a good company all of your life and retire with a solid pension.
- Count on Social Security to pay for half of your retirement.

Those were the days! Today, very few have equity built up in their homes and might have difficulty selling if they did. Buy-and-hold has proved to be less than desirable during volatile market cycles. Fixed-income securities and CDs are not paying very attractive rates. Pensions are going away, along with the certainty of Social Security, for many younger workers.

I believe now more than ever that personal, caring service from a qualified, experienced financial professional is as important to meeting retirement needs as high-fiber granola, antioxidant-rich blueberries, and skim milk is to aging well. My team and I stand ready to help you and those you care about meet those challenges. According to Vanguard, "an experienced financial advisor provides customized portfolio management and discipline which can better position you to reach your long-term investment objectives. A good financial advisor will also build a relationship with you that goes beyond traditional financial planning and results in a more valuable financial life-planning approach" (*"Learn How Your Financial Advisor Adds Value,"* The Vanguard Group, 2011). I could not say it any better myself.

RETIREMENT RISK #1: LONGEVITY

The most common risk that most people fail to address is that of longevity, which is funny because most people think they are going to live forever! This really hit home a couple of years ago during our annual Elite Conference, where the top advisors of the firm gather to share ideas and learn from industry thought leaders how to serve clients more effectively. There was a panel of high–net worth investors on hand to evaluate some of the advisor's answers to commonly asked questions. When the subject of retirement planning came up, one of the top advisors said these investors should be prepared to have their money last at least another twenty years past the normal retirement age of sixty-five. The response from the majority of the focus group was laughter! They could not grasp the concept that longer life spans meant their money had to last longer. Well, guess what?

From the Fall 2011 newsletter:

> ### Living Long
>
> Since I brought up the subject of longevity, it may be interesting to know that many experts believe it is possible that with better diets, more exercise, and significant scientific advances, some people alive today could expect to live to 150 or beyond. A growing number of forward-thinking scientists, doctors, researchers, biogeneticists and nano-technologists insist that significantly longer life spans are scientifically achievable. Federal funding for research into "the biology of aging" has been running at about $2.4 billion a year.
>
> Anti-aging researchers at genetics labs of major universities have found that mice and flies can switch on an anti-aging mechanism when put on certain diets. Researchers have successfully lengthened the lives of lab mice by 20 percent by boosting natural antioxidants. Recent breakthroughs like "smart drugs" that target tumors or their blood supplies also offer some encouragement. Proponents of

extra-long living see a day when nanotechnology will allow molecular robots to run through our bodies continually making repairs. I wonder where all of these people will live, and which bank will offer the first 150-year mortgage!

From the Summer 2012 newsletter:

RETIREMENT RISKOLOGY

Thanks to a combination of medical advances, better nutrition, and healthier lifestyles, we are living longer than ever these days. Some 80,000 Americans will turn 100 by 2020. By the year 2030, that number will climb to 200,000—and many will include you (Census.gov, 2009)! This good news increases the risk of running out of money. You and your spouse may need a source of income for as many years in retirement as you did when you where working.

From the Summer 2005 newsletter:

BAFFLED BOOMERS' LAST PAYCHECKS

As the 65 million baby boomers begin to turn sixty at a rate of one every ten seconds over the next fifteen years, study after study reveals that precious few of them have a clear, quantified picture of their retirement income. Even though they are the most affluent generation of Americans who ever lived, they are woefully unprepared for life after their final paycheck. More often than not, this lack of preparation is not from stupidity or laziness, but from a genuine fear of finding out just how far behind they are in their retirement funding.

Do not be one of those who get to that point in life unprepared and without a plan to succeed! Prepare to make this phase of life as enjoyable and worry-free as possible.

Your plan should include what I believe to be the seven essentials for a successful retirement:

- Proper Diversification/Asset Allocation/Risk Management
- Access to Top Money Managers, Funds, and Strategies
- Periodic Rebalancing—Buy Low and Sell High Systematically
- Ongoing Due Diligence and Monitoring
- Principle Protection for Heirs
- Income Protection/Guaranteed Minimum Income for Life
- Upside Potential/Inflation Protection

RETIREMENT RISK #2: SEQUENCE OF RETURNS

If you had one million dollars and needed $50,000 (5 percent) per year to live, you might think that investing in a mutual fund (or index fund, or any investment program) that had an average rate of return of 7 percent per year over a long period of time would allow you to live forever and never run out of money. However, even the best funds do not earn their average rate of return every year. The returns are uneven and include both positive and negative periods. This is an important concept, so I will bore you with the following chart to emphasize my point.

(Data based on two thirty-one-year periods ending on December 31, 1998 and 2008, respectively. Each portfolio assumes a first-year 5 percent withdrawal that was subsequently adjusted for actual inflation. Each portfolio also assumes a 60 percent stock/40 percent bond allocation, rebalanced annually. Stocks are represented by the S&P 500. The Standard & Poor's 500 Index is an unmanaged group of large company stocks. It is not possible to invest directly in an index. Bonds are represented by the annualized yields of long-term Treasuries [ten-plus years maturity]. Inflation is represented by changes to the historical CPI. Past performance does not guarantee future results.)

| | | Mr. Smith | | | Ms. Jones | |
| | | Investment: $100,000 Stocks 60% \| Bonds 40% Retired 1/1/1969 – Annual withdrawals: $5,000 | | | Investment: $100,000 Stocks 60% \| Bonds 40% Retired 1/1/1979 – Annual withdrawals: $5,000 | |
Age	Year	ROR	Year-end value	Year	ROR	Year-end value
65	1969	-2.6%	$92,168	1979	14.7%	$109,172
66	1970	5.3%	$91,449	1980	23.9%	$128,899
67	1971	10.5%	$95,219	1981	3.4%	$126,282
68	1972	12.9%	$101,447	1982	16.6%	$139,848
69	1973	-6.6%	$88,410	1983	16.6%	$155,426
70	1974	-12.6%	$70,219	1984	7.3%	$158,880
71	1975	25.1%	$80,085	1985	22.0%	$185,630
72	1976	16.5%	$85,107	1986	13.9%	$203,223
73	1977	-2.4%	$74,324	1987	5.7%	$206,232
74	1978	6.3%	$69,660	1988	12.2%	$222,537
75	1979	14.7%	$69,487	1989	22.1%	$262,402
76	1980	23.9%	$74,222	1990	1.2%	$255,753
77	1981	3.4%	$63,670	1991	20.8%	$298,808
78	1982	16.6%	$60,391	1992	6.1%	$306,574
79	1983	16.6%	$56,145	1993	7.3%	$318,026
80	1984	7.3%	$45,480	1994	2.0%	$313,351
81	1985	22.0%	$40,198	1995	24.6%	$378,884
82	1986	13.9%	$30,286	1996	16.3%	$429,072
83	1987	5.7%	$15,941	1997	21.1%	$507,502
84	1988	12.2%	$1,176	1998	19.1%	$592,094
85	1989	22.1%	Exhausted	1999	14.3%	$664,249
86	1990	1.2%	Exhausted	2000	-0.8%	$645,969
87	1991	20.8%	Exhausted	2001	-3.8%	$608,120
88	1992	6.1%	Exhausted	2002	-9.3%	$538,413
89	1993	7.3%	Exhausted	2003	18.9%	$626,319
90	1994	2.0%	Exhausted	2004	8.2%	$663,790
91	1995	24.6%	Exhausted	2005	3.8%	$674,761
92	1996	16.3%	Exhausted	2006	11.2%	$735,149
93	1997	21.1%	Exhausted	2007	6.1%	$764,278
94	1998	19.1%	Exhausted	2008	-20.5%	$591,402
		Average ROR 10.5%			Average ROR 9.6%	

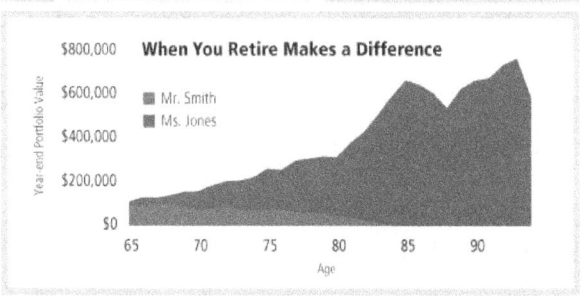

When You Retire Makes a Difference

To further illustrate the point, consider the example below from the Winter 2008 newsletter:

SEQUENCE OF EVENTS

When I was in high school, my primary goal as the quarterback for Collingswood High School was to win the Brooks-Irvine Award as the top football player in South Jersey. My other goal was to beat Haddonfield every time I played them. After that, I dreamed of going on to be the quarterback for Notre Dame. Years before, my father had won the Brooks Award as the Lineman of the Year when he played for Collingswood High (Irvine was his coach and was added to the award later). His team's only loss was to Haddonfield. I wanted to follow in his footsteps and avenge his only loss. My hope for going to Notre Dame was that the quarterback at that time was a little guy named Joe Theismann, who was a runner-up for the Heisman Trophy. He had followed another smallish quarterback, three-time All-American Terry Hanratty. I figured if they could do it, so could I.

Each year we beat Haddonfield. During my senior year I had the game of my life against them, throwing three touchdowns and scoring one myself. That should have gotten me at least Player of the Week and put me on track for Player of the Year. The next week changed everything. We were killing the other team and I was having another big day when I took a shot to the thigh early in the second half. I finished the game, but I would never play again. There would be no Player of the Year Award and no scholarship to Notre Dame.

Meanwhile, Joe Theismann went on to lead the Washington Redskins to a win in Super Bowl XVII and an appearance in Super Bowl XVIII. He would go on to set several Redskins franchise records. He was the NFL's MVP in 1983 and played two Pro Bowl games, earning the player of the game award in the second game. Theismann's career ended on November 18, 1985, when he suffered a gruesome compound fracture of his leg while being sacked by New York Giants linebackers Lawrence Taylor and Harry Carson during a Monday Night Football game telecast. He never played again.

Okay, I certainly would not suggest that I would have gone on to Notre Dame, the NFL, and the Super Bowl had I not gotten hurt (although anything is possible!). I am also not complaining, because my life has been pretty good so far without a Super Bowl ring. What I am suggesting, though, is that Joe Theismann would not have gone on to football greatness if he had sustained his career-ending injury during his senior year of high school like I did. This allows me to segue into a discussion of the perils of the "sequence of returns" when it comes to investments.

Sequence of Returns

Like dominos, return sequence, or the order of which your investments' returns occur, can have a dramatic impact on your retirement income—or, more importantly, on its ability to last.

Its effects are lessened when assets are accumulating. Long-term return averages can still be met, and accumulation goals can still be achieved over time. However, once an investor begins to withdraw assets, return sequence can devastate their retirement plan. If a portfolio enjoys positive returns during the early years of withdrawals, the funds may last well beyond one's life expectancy. But if a retirement portfolio experiences a decline within the first few years of retirement, the funds could run out well before the need for income runs out. This is true even if the average annual rate of return is identical over the long term for both portfolios. The sequence of returns is the only difference, but it could make all of the difference. If Joe Theismann had gotten injured early in his career and I had lasted until late in mine, he might be explaining the phenomenon and I might be doing color commentary for Monday Night Football.

RETIREMENT RISK #3: REVERSE DOLLAR-COST AVERAGING

During the accumulation stage prior to retirement, investors making systematic deposits into an investment portfolio will typically benefit from "dollar-cost averaging." This benefit results from nothing more than taking advantage of periodic drops in the price of an investment being systematically purchased. During these periods of share price decline, the investor is getting more shares for the dollars being invested. Once an investor retires and begins to take systematic withdrawals from their retirement portfolio, any periodic declines in the price of these shares, now being sold to cover expenses, become detrimental. Retirees look to generate a certain amount of dollars to pay expenses, so when the share prices of the investments in the portfolio decline, the retiree has to sell more shares to raise the dollars needed. This is reverse dollar-cost averaging. The long-term effect is that retirees get less out of their investments than historical rates might suggest because they take money out on a regular basis, and the periodic withdrawals in a low market leave permanent damage.

From the Winter 2012 newsletter:

THE TUCK RULE

In January 2012, for the fifth time in ten years, Tom Brady led the New England Patriots into the Super Bowl. Ten years ago the Patriots were coming off of a dismal 5–11 season under first-year head coach Bill Belichick. A young Tom Brady was filling in for injured quarterback Drew Bledsoe, and there was no dynasty yet. The Patriots reached the AFC divisional playoff game against the Oakland Raiders, played in the snow at Foxboro Stadium. With time running out and the Patriots down by three, blitzing Raiders cornerback Charles Woodson sacked Brady, causing a fumble which was recovered by the Raiders. All the Raiders had to do at that point was run out the clock to advance to the Super Bowl.

However, officials reviewed the play and, citing the "tuck rule," determined that Brady's arm was moving forward, thus making it an incomplete pass. The original call was overturned and the ball was given back to the Patriots, who kicked a field goal to tie the game and eventually win it in overtime. The Patriots went on to win the Super Bowl that year, and the dynasty was born. The Belichick/Brady duo went on to win more games (and counting) than any coach/quarterback tandem in NFL history and won back-to-back Super Bowls in 2003 and 2004.

I have watched that play about a hundred times, and I do not care what anybody says—it was a fumble. Of course, nobody cares what I think, but what if the original call stood? Tom Brady would have gone into the off-season as the bum who fumbled the game away, and we may never have heard from him again. The dynasty might have belonged to the Raiders, Drew Bledsoe may have returned to the starting role rather than getting traded the next year, and Bill Belichick may not be regarded as a coaching genius.

Reversal of Fortune

Another phenomenon that affects most retirees is that of reverse dollar-cost averaging. Reverse dollar-cost averaging, like dollar-cost averaging, involves a fixed dollar amount of money during a specified time period. With dollar-cost averaging, you invest a fixed amount of money every year. With reverse dollar-cost averaging, you withdraw a certain amount of money every year. The most common reason for retirees to withdraw a fixed amount of money every month is to meet living expenses and spending needs.

Obviously, the more cash you withdraw from your investment accounts, the less money you will have working for you and potentially growing in those accounts. Many, if not most, retirees making systematic withdrawals find that their retirement accounts get smaller and smaller over time and may even be depleted. A number of retirees have been surprised to learn that reverse dollar-cost averaging can be dangerous, even during those periods of time when the stock market is rising.

There are several ways to combat the effects of sequence-of-returns risk and reverse dollar-cost averaging. This first is simply not to spend too much money! I know this sounds ridiculous, but the biggest issue I have with many clients is their desire to withdraw more than a reasonable rate of return from their investments. Or, they take big chunks out and still expect to continue withdrawing the same monthly amount from less money. When money is withdrawn, there is less money to draw from in the future. So, if you want your money to last, leave it invested!

Another way to overcome these risks is to diversify your portfolio and diversify your sources of income. Proper diversification, including cash, fixed income, and equities, should reduce the volatility of your portfolio and serve to mute the effects of wild swings in the financial markets. By including short-term, highly liquid investments, the retiree is not under duress to sell, which can be especially beneficial in years when both fixed income and equities are undervalued in the market. Finally, you should consider guaranteed sources of income that you cannot outlive. This source of income should complement the increasing streams of income that high-quality dividend-paying equities can provide, rather than replace them. I will discuss this later.

RETIREMENT RISK # 4: COMPLACENCY

In his best-selling book, *What Got You Here May Not Get You There*, author Marshall Goldsmith asks the question, "What's holding you back? Your hard work is paying off. You are doing well in your field. But there is something standing between you and the next level of achievement. Perhaps one small flaw—a behavior you barely even recognize—is the only thing that's keeping you from where you want to be."

I am asking the same question. I suggest the one thing that holds back many retirees from a financially successful retirement is complacency, often evidenced by a concentrated position that they refuse to sell. Managing a retirement portfolio is entirely different from accumulating one. You cannot hope that the things you were doing before will be all right when you no longer have the capacity to replenish your portfolio to make up for mistakes. You may have to change. I know that is hard for many people, but to resist change is to take too much risk into retirement.

From the Fall 2011 newsletter:

WATCHING THE CLOCK

In the summer of 2011, before our elected officials argued about a debt ceiling compromise and our debt rating was downgraded, the country was united in cheering for the US women's soccer team as they advanced in the World Cup. Team USA had captured the hearts of Americans for their creativity, dazzling plays, and free spirit. After a rousing victory over powerhouse Brazil, they hoped to become the first squad to win the women's World Cup three times. Secretary of State Hilary Clinton even spoke by phone with the team before the final game, wishing the players good luck against underdog Japan and telling them how proud America was of them.

The Americans controlled most of the action for the majority of the game. However, they could not capitalize on their early dominance. Finally, midway through the second half, the United States scored, only to give up an easy goal with nine minutes left in regulation. Victory again was within reach when the girls scored again in extra time. As I watched, I became increasingly nervous and frustrated as the Japanese never gave up and the US team seemed to grow more tired by the minute. Then the Japanese scored again, just before the end of extra time, forcing the game to be decided by penalty shots. The United States was stunned as the final penalty shot went in and Japan was the world champion.

South Jersey's Carli Lloyd described her thoughts during the final ten minutes as she and her teammates were trying to hold onto the lead. She said she kept looking at the clock, hoping for time to run out before Japan could score again (Courier-Post, July 17, 2011). I sensed the same thing as I watched the game on TV. The United States seemed to be trying not to lose, waiting for the clock to run out, rather than continuing to play for the win. It cost them the World Cup.

Every Day Counts

What does that soccer game have to do with financial planning? A well-thought-out financial plan can be ruined if we lose our discipline and start watching the clock, thinking that we can just cruise along, hoping that outside events do not ruin our plan. Whether we are in the asset accumulation (growth) or asset distribution (income) phase, success requires the same planning, implementation, and monitoring every day for the whole game (life). We must stay diligent vs. lazy, be tactical vs. buy-and-hold, and maintain diversification by avoiding concentrated positions. The economy, interest rates, and financial markets are changing more frequently than ever before. Your financial plan should be flexible enough to respond to those changes and keep you on course. Looking at the clock and trying to hold on may cost you your financial goals.

Good to Great

Avoiding concentrated positions is important to your financial health. You may wonder how it can be bad to hold onto shares of a company that has allowed you to accumulate wealth over the years, especially if it is a good or even great company. *Good to Great* by Jim Collins is one of the most read business books, having sold millions of copies since it came out in 2001. It still sells over 300,000 copies a year. The book focuses on eleven companies that were just okay and then transformed themselves into greatness—where greatness is defined as a sustained period where the stock dramatically outperformed the market and its competitors.

These companies also, according to the book, had the sorts of characteristics which made them "built to last." One of the companies was Fannie Mae, which not only has since gone to zero but continues to cost taxpayers untold billions of dollars. Another, Circuit City, also went to zero. Yet another, Wells Fargo, lost over 60 percent of its value and cut its dividend by over 60 percent during the financial crisis in 2008. The stock has since recovered over half of its decline, but if you were counting on the dividend for income, you are still suffering. So do not get caught watching the clock while one position becomes a large part of your wealth, putting your portfolio at risk.

A concentrated position is a huge risk that is not necessary or desirable for someone at, near, or into retirement. To me, this is the ultimate in complacency. There are many reasons that people have these large positions as a percentage of their total portfolio, and a concentrated portfolio often is a way to amass wealth. However, once one becomes dependent on their portfolio as their source of future income, emotional or sentimental attachments to large positions is not advisable (to put it mildly). Believe me—the companies are not emotional or sentimental about you! Few stocks, no matter how prized, have proven immune to a drastic turn of events. Shareholders of numerous large and once-prestigious companies like TWA, Magnavox, Enron, Singer, Pan Am, WorldCom, Wang, and Lucent have suffered immensely from poor management decisions, overexpansion, new competition, or unethical business practices. Many large positions carry with them huge, potentially taxable gains. The specifics of the strategies to reduce or eliminate these positions while minimizing the tax bite are beyond the scope of this book, but some ways to consider would be staged sales, hedging techniques, charitable remainder trusts, and exchange funds.

RETIREMENT RISK #5: THE BLACK SWAN EVENT

You can plan, save, invest properly, and still be blindsided by an event that is completely unexpected. This is commonly referred to as a "black swan" event, so named because black swans are so rare. A black swan is an unpredictable, uncommon, but nevertheless high-impact event. The black swan event lies outside the realm of common experience, and nothing in our past experience points to its possibility. A black swan is that million-to-one chance that statisticians said would never happen *because* it was a million-to-one chance.

When the black swan strikes, it has a massive impact. It could be terrorist activity around the world, or talk of Ebola coming into our country. It could be a financial crisis and subsequent stock market crash that wipes out *billions*, or a tsunami or earthquake over a major city. Not only is the qualitative nature of the black swan outside our regular experience (meaning we can't see it coming), so is its sheer size—a single event can dominate over all other factors.

The unpredictability and magnitude of such an event is illustrated in the Summer 2011 newsletter:

Black Swan Events

Over the summer of 2011, I was helping out with my grandson Carson's Little League team. He had a pretty good season, but his team was like the Bad News Bears. They lost their first six games and only won three games all season. Every team qualified for the playoffs, which was a double elimination tournament, so I figured two games and we would be done. I was more than surprised when, a week later, we were playing in the championship game with four playoff wins (one more win than we had all season). During our playoff run we had several kids get their first hits all year, and others made some plays in the field that were truly amazing. The game ended with Carson standing on third base as the tying run. He had hit a double and stolen third, even though he runs like he has a piano on his back. We had exceeded everyone's expectations by so much, including our own, that it did not matter whether we won the championship or not. The team was happy, and we had a fun week. By contrast, there were four other teams that had really good seasons, but exited the playoffs deeply disappointed. Getting knocked out by our team was truly a black swan event.

As an investor, sometimes you do everything by the book and have a good season only to be stunned by unpredictable outside events. If a great season could automatically guarantee a successful playoff run, then the teams who played the best all year would not have been disappointed—but that is why they play the games! When a well-thought-out, properly implemented retirement investment program is blindsided by a black swan event, it would be nice if there was some way to lock in the previous performance and guarantee the income for life that the program was designed to provide.

From the Fall 2010 newsletter:

> Forty-eight-year-old Scottish singer Susan Boyle, who was discovered on the television show "Britain's Got Talent," has captivated hearts around the globe with her debut album, "I Dreamed a Dream," hitting the top of the charts in the United States, the United Kingdom, Ireland, Canada, and New Zealand. It is the fastest-selling UK album of all time, selling 411,820 copies in one week. In the States, the album sold more than 710,000 copies in its first week and is now eight times platinum in Australia. It is expected to be the highest-selling album of the year in several countries. "I Dreamed a Dream" was also the biggest pre-ordered album in retailer Amazon.com's history (perthnow.com).

Boyle's audition for "Britain's Got Talent" in April 2009, during which she sang "I Dreamed a Dream" from the musical "Les Miserables," became an Internet sensation. More than 300 million people watched the clip on YouTube. When the humble, plain-looking Boyle took the stage, she was greeted with snickers and sneers, but she left the stage to a standing ovation from the audience and judges, many of whom were brought to tears by her beautiful rendition. She has since become a cult hero, an example for anyone who has a dream.

I was watching "I Dreamed a Dream: The Susan Boyle Story" last week on television and getting caught up in her truly inspirational story. I was thinking how appropriate it was that her rags-to-riches story was launched by such an uplifting song about dreaming a dream! But then I listened closer to the words of the song.

> *I had a dream my life would be*
> *So different from this hell I'm living*
> *So different now from what it seemed*
> *Now life has killed the dream I dreamed!*

I dug a little deeper and found out that the character in the musical who sang the song, Fantine, was alone, unemployed, and destitute. The dream was a nightmare.

Planning for Reality

Financial planning is a useful exercise to help people realize their hopes, dreams, and life goals. A well-structured plan can help reduce uncertainty and provide the confidence that your actions today can help you achieve your goals for tomorrow. That sounds pretty good, doesn't it? But life does not always go like we planned. That is why I believe that any plan should consider all possible outcomes and be flexible enough to allow for when world changes and one's needs change. And while the plan is very important, it is the execution that is critical. When outside events threaten to turn your dream into a nightmare, the advice and counsel of a qualified and dedicated financial professional becomes essential.

RETIREMENT RISK #6: NOT PAYING FOR PROTECTION—AGAIN

Twenty-five years ago, defined benefit plans were workers' primary source of guaranteed retirement income. These plans required workers to make almost no important financial decisions before retirement. The company would enroll all eligible workers, make contributions, and make all investment decisions, ultimately providing a lifetime benefit at retirement. The worker's only real choice was when to collect benefits.

When 401(k) plans began to spread in the 1980s, they were viewed as a supplement to guaranteed income pensions and Social Security. Guaranteed income is projected to cover a decreasing share of retirement income, leaving households with increased responsibility for their retirement. Americans' increased reliance on defined contribution pension plans and personal savings raises serious sustainability challenges. Many Americans will have to reduce their standard of living significantly due to fluctuating investment returns and the probability of spending more time in retirement. Middle-income Americans entering retirement without a guaranteed source of income beyond Social Security will have an even higher risk of outliving their financial assets than current retirees.

How can you mitigate that risk? Unfortunately, you have to pay someone to either reduce the risk or take on the risk. You can pay a financial advisor to help you diversify properly and monitor your portfolio in an effort to reduce the overall risk. I think I have covered that enough. You can also pay for protection by transferring the risk of a market implosion or black swan event to a third party who will guarantee your income for the rest of your life. That income may go up if the markets perform well, but it will not go down or end until you are gone. This protection is not free, hence the "paying."

From the Fall 2000 newsletter, continued:

PLANNING TO SUCCEED

There is always a degree of systematic risk to any portfolio, which cannot be diversified away or eliminated through superior information and research. Principal protection for heirs and income protection for you and your spouse are available only at a cost. It is surprising how low that cost can be, especially considering the cost of not having it when you or your heirs need it.

Pain of Regret

I have had the good fortune to see most of my son Jonathon's baseball games. However, when he was eleven, I missed his first home run because I was with a client doing a portfolio review. I have a picture in my office of him crossing the plate after a home run he hit in high school, which I really like because he is being greeted by all of his good buddies on the team. I missed that home run, too, because I was hosting a client appreciation dinner that night. I missed these special moments because I was building my business by providing caring financial management for families "on the grow" (believe me—I saw more games than I missed). If I would have been there with him, would I regret now that I did not spend more time on my business?

Which is worse: the pain of sacrifice or the pain of regret? If you sacrifice all of your life to save for retirement, but do not make it, do you regret missing out on some of the pleasures of life? Then again, if you save nothing and have no money for retirement and have to work until you die, do you regret not sacrificing while you were young? What if you saved and accumulated a retirement nest egg over your working lifetime, only to have your portfolio severely damaged by a bear market right when your family needed it to manage without you? Or the money was gone before you were? Would you regret not paying a little extra to guarantee the accumulated principal for your heirs, or provide a minimum guaranteed pension while still participating in the upside potential of the markets?

Some products provide a guaranteed income that is fixed for the life of you and/or your spouse beginning immediately. Some products allow you to "buy" a stream of income you cannot outlive that will begin at a future date. Some provide the ability to grow with the market, either through an index or through investing in sub-accounts. Suffice it to say that there are many ways to transfer the risk of a black swan event or a poor sequence of returns to a third party, usually an insurance company. None of these are free, and all are subject to the claims-paying ability of the insurance company making the guarantee.

These products, or a combination of them, are appropriate for many people in conjunction with the diversified portfolio of cash, fixed income, and equities discussed earlier. However, read the fine print and ask a lot of questions. Some of the fees are hidden in the form of "participation rates" and caps on the returns. Other fees are more transparent, but only if you read the marketing material. The fees and expenses may be worth the peace of mind that you will have a source of income that you cannot outlive no matter what market conditions exist, and no matter how long you live. But you should know what they are!

From the Spring 2005 newsletter:

My Generation

It has been more than forty years since The Who first sang "My Generation," the rock anthem claiming a desire to "die before I get old." Unfortunately, some of the members of the band did die before they got old. The remaining members, however, are still performing and playing that song to aging baby boomers who are now more concerned with outliving their money than dying before they get old.

In 2005 I reached the half-century mark. With two kids married, two in college, one who is growing fast, and two grandchildren, I look around and think "What happened?" I never bought that Datsun 240Z I wanted, and now I walk right past the sports cars to look at minivans. I no longer am investing to get rich, but to provide sufficient income that I cannot outlive.

As the generation that once drove the "magic bus" now enjoys senior citizen discounts to ride SEPTA buses, the focus has shifted from revolution to a revelation that our money will have to work harder than ever before to provide sufficient income to meet rising costs of living. The 76 million baby boomers born between 1946 and 1964 are now shifting from an accumulation phase to a distribution phase. Sixty-five percent of these boomers are not sure if they will have enough money to live comfortably in retirement. They are beginning to realize their income will need to be stretched over twenty to thirty years. During that time, even moderate inflation can erode purchasing power by over 50 percent.

The Wonder Years

As more boomers approach or enter retirement, they are looking at their lives and asking "What happened?" They're wondering why they did so little to prepare for retirement income. Many are finding, among other things, that many expenses, such as healthcare, take up more of their income then they had planned. With interest rates still close to forty-year lows, yields on traditional income-producing investments like CDs and bonds are not enough to meet those expenses. Many people are overly conservative with their investments because of poor past performance or because they believe they should be conservative in their later years. So even though they may need the growth and higher total return potential of equities, they avoid them. Eighty-two percent of boomers say they would be interested in a financial product that could provide growth potential with guaranteed protection and income.

INCOME FOR LIFE, PART 2—INSTRUMENTAL

Is there a financial product that can provide the growth potential of equities with guaranteed protection and income? Yes, here comes yet another discussion of variable annuities with living benefits. Most living benefits assure that you will always have money coming in, no matter how long you live. These optional features are designed to help provide a predictable level of future income regardless of investment performance or actual account value. The most popular, and the one I usually recommend where appropriate, is the guaranteed minimum income benefit (GMIB).

Most GMIBs use two separate income bases from which a guaranteed income stream can be calculated. The first is a compounding income base. This protects against a bear market by offering a floor, or minimum rate of return, which is compounded annually. This income base allows an investor to know in advance what the lowest possible guaranteed income stream will be regardless of market conditions or investment performance. The second is the highest anniversary income base. This base steps up periodically to lock in the gains of a bull market. This serves to protect an investor from volatile markets by basing retirement income on the highest account value on any prior contract anniversary. Both bases are adjusted for any additions or withdrawals, and they require a minimum holding period.

All guarantees are based upon the claims-paying ability of the issuing insurance company. Also, these optional benefit riders are not free. My job is to help investors understand the cost relative to the benefits and guarantees and to make informed decisions. Of course, the GMIB will be moot if the investment returns exceed the guaranteed compounding income rate and the account is at or near the highest anniversary value at the time income is desired. There are many other bells and whistles available with these financial planning products.

From the Fall 2006 newsletter:

Gidget Turns Sixty

On November 6, 2006, Sally Field, who burst onto the scene in 1965 as Frances Elizabeth "Gidget" Lawrence, will turn sixty. (Some movie buffs may insist that Sandra Dee is the true Gidget—born Alexandra Cymboliak Zuck in 1942, she turned sixty-four this year.) Ms. Field also entertained us as Sister Bertrille the Flying Nun, Norma Rae, Mrs. Doubtfire's wife, Forrest Gump's mother, and more recently as Maggie Wyczenski, Nurse Abby Lockhart's mother on ER. She will join Sly Stone and the 77 million baby boomers that begin to cross over into the over-sixty club this year. Thanks to medical advances and an overall better standard of living, she, Sly, and the rest of that group can expect to live longer than their parents or grandparents. While most people would agree that this is good news, longer life spans can create planning challenges when it comes to retirement and health care.

According to the US Census Bureau, there are currently 35 million Americans age sixty-five and older, and this number is projected to double by 2030. Also, the number of people living into their 80s and 90s is expected to increase. The possibility of spending two, three, or even four decades in retirement, coupled with the decline of traditional lifetime pensions, means that your nest egg has never been more crucial. And since there is a risk that Social Security will provide reduced benefits down the road (the program is expected to be insolvent by 2041 if no fixes are made), you may need to take some action now.

Your investment portfolio will likely be one of your major sources of retirement income. As such, it is important to make sure that your level of risk, your choice of investment vehicles, and your asset allocation are appropriate considering your long-term objectives. While you don't want to lose your investment principal, you also don't want to lose out to inflation. A review of your investment portfolio is essential in determining whether your money will last.

Paying for Protection

Living benefits, death benefits, accumulation benefits, withdrawal benefits—these are all features of variable annuity products, which are designed to provide principal protection for your heirs or a minimum guaranteed pension while still participating in the upside potential of the markets, or both. These benefits are subject to the claims-paying ability of the issuing insurance companies and are available only at a cost. Protection is not free—even Don Vito Corleone needed Luca Brasi—but it may be an offer you can't refuse.

Remember, these guaranteed income products should not replace a diversified portfolio of stocks, bonds, and cash carefully designed to provide a source of income that will meet your needs and keep pace with inflation and rising medical costs. However, used as a complement to your investment portfolio, these products may be appropriate as a form of longevity insurance and protection from black swan events.

IN SUMMARY

Avoiding the investor no-no's (no plan, no process, no idea, no purpose) and biggest mistakes (great expectations, fighting the last war, believing the current hype, not paying for protection, and other stuff) will allow you to accumulate wealth over the course of your working career. Recognizing and addressing the special risks surrounding retirement—longevity, sequence of returns, reverse dollar-cost averaging, complacency, black swan events, and not paying for protection again—will put you on the path to making work optional in your later years. You can then focus on doing what you *want* to do instead of what you *have* to do.

CHAPTER FIVE

The Best Investment

The ideal investment should have certain characteristics. It should not require a large initial payment. In fact, it should allow you to create something from nothing. It should be low risk, with unlimited return potential. The investment should provide a return beyond one's life and into future generations. The return should be far greater than a financial return. The future of any family, organization, or civilization depends on the next generation, so it stands to reason that the most important investment we can make is to prepare that next generation.

Proverbs 22:6 tells us to "Train up a child in the way he should go, and when he is old he will not depart from it." We should not educate children to be rich, but educate them to be happy. That way, when they grow up they will know the *value* of things, not the price. If we pour ourselves into others, the lessons we teach them through both our words and actions will live on and produce a return for generations to come.

Anything we can do to give others, and especially young people, hope for the future represents the best investment we can make. Once you are successful financially, you can contribute to causes that ease peoples' pain or provide them encouragement or give them hope. Once you have made work optional, you can invest time into causes or people that result in the same comfort, encouragement, or hope.

Where hope lives, lives can change for the better and futures can be improved. I have talked a lot about mistakes. Mistakes can hurt. What makes us better and gives the people around us hope is to forgive others their mistakes and show the compassion and grace that God has shown to us. The apostle Paul says in 1 Corinthians 8 that "knowledge puffs up, while love builds up." Loving people like there is no tomorrow is never a mistake—but in reality, there is a tomorrow. Yesterday ended last night. If we put the mistakes of yesterday behind us and use today to make life better for those around us, we are sowing seeds for growth tomorrow.

I hope that my stewardship helps my clients—past, present, and future—to avoid the mistakes discussed in the previous pages and make work optional. I hope this book has helped you, and I hope that my children and grandchildren will someday pass along some of the lessons I have tried to teach them, just like my father and mother taught me. If so, then my investment into them will pay dividends for generations to come.

www.ingramcontent.com/pod-product-compliance
Lightning Source LLC
Chambersburg PA
CBHW051713170526
45167CB00002B/638